COME DRINK AT THE FOUNT

Come Drink at the Fount

Introducing the Carmelite Authors

EDMOND CULLINAN TOC

VERITAS

First published 2021 by
Veritas Publications
7–8 Lower Abbey Street
Dublin 1
Ireland
publications@veritas.ie
www.veritas.ie

ISBN 978 1 80097 010 6

Imprimatur: ✠ Bishop Alphonsus Cullinan, Bishop of
Waterford and Lismore

10 9 8 7 6 5 4 3 2 1

Cover design by Colette Dower, Veritas Publications
Printed in the Republic of Ireland by SPRINT-print, Dublin

Lines from 'Absence' from
The Collected Poems by Elizabeth Jennings (Carcanet Press),
reproduced by permission of David Higham Associates.

*Veritas books are printed on paper made from the wood pulp of
managed forests. For every tree felled, at least one tree is planted,
thereby renewing natural resources.*

Dedicated to Our Lady of Mount Carmel
and for Fr Seán Casey

*The water that I will give will become in them a spring
of water gushing up to eternal life.*
– John 4:14

*With this other fount, the water comes from its own
source, which is God.*
– Saint Teresa of Ávila, *The Interior Castle*, IV, 1, 4

Contents

Acknowledgements

Saint Augustine tells us that the human heart is restless until it rests in God. This expresses well the situation today. There is a great restlessness abroad. Although many do not realise it, at a deep level people are thirsting for God. The various traditions of Christian spirituality are ways of responding to this restlessness and this thirst. Carmelite spirituality is particularly accessible because it has been expressed in the writings of very gifted women and men. My purpose in presenting this book is to introduce the principal Carmelite authors, so that readers will be motivated to explore the writings further themselves. They will find there a rich source of spirituality.

I was first introduced to the Carmelite authors by the nuns of St Joseph's Monastery, Tallow, County Waterford. I am grateful to the sisters for their example and prayers. I was able to imbibe Carmelite spirituality further during my many visits to the Retreat and Spirituality Centre at the Carmelite Friary, Kinsale, County Cork. I would like to thank the friars there for their hospitality and for sharing their insights with me. I thank especially Fr Stan Hession O. Carm., Director of the Third Order.

I thank the Prior General, Fr Míceál O'Neill O. Carm., for doing me the honour of writing the foreword for this book.

I thank Bishop Alphonsus Cullinan for his caring support for my ministry since he became Bishop of Waterford and Lismore, and for the encouragement he has given me in my writing.

The impetus for the present book came from the members of the Focolare Word of Life group who met monthly at the Cathedral of the Most Holy Trinity, Waterford, when I was ministering there. I thank them for their friendship, support and encouragement.

Since I contacted Veritas Publications with a view to having the book published, I have found the staff to be unfailingly courteous, helpful and professional. I would like to thank Denise Murphy, Pamela McLoughlin, Emma O'Donoghue and Colette Dower for their work and for bringing the book to its readers.

Edmond Cullinan TOC
Pontifical Irish College, Rome
8 September 2021, Feast of the Nativity of Our Lady

Foreword

Whoever opens the pages of this book by Fr Edmond Cullinan will find a very attractive presentation of Carmelite saints and their spirituality. It may be dipped into at different times, read chapter by chapter, or used by a study or reflection group. All will find it very helpful. Edmond gives us a selection of the principal Carmelite saints. As it turns out, all of them belong to the Discalced Carmelite tradition. This strikes me as significant because the familiarity that Edmond has with these saints – bearing in mind that he is a member of the O. Carm. Third Order – is an indication of how all of Carmel finds in these saints and their writings everything that speaks of Carmel, its traditions and its spirituality.

Here we have saints who followed the Carmelite Rule, lived in community, celebrated the liturgy and devoted themselves to the quest for union with God. Here are the saints that discovered that our relationship with God is not something we can manufacture. It is initiated and completed by the love of God, drawing the pure and humble to himself.

Beginning with St Teresa of Ávila, we see how the quest for God passes through the humanity of Jesus and is discovered in humility and friendship. In John of the Cross, we see the beauty of the quest for God in the soul that goes out, fired by love's longings, to discover a God who has already wounded the soul in love. John plots the steps along the way that pass through the dark night of the senses and the dark night of the spirit until union is complete. In this movement, God draws every soul to himself and moves it to ever-deeper levels of motivation until it reaches the deepest level – God himself.

Lawrence of the Resurrection is presented by Edmond in a way that is very easy to follow. Knowing that God is present all the time, anyone seeking God has only to be attentive, in prayer and outside of prayer. Thérèse of Lisieux appeals to the author for many reasons, among them her great love for priests and missionaries. Thérèse is important also because of her attention to God's love acting in her life. In her discernment, she discovers that her vocation is to be love in the heart of the Church, her mother.

Finally, of the many angles Edmond might have taken in presenting Edith Stein, he chose her regard for liturgy, from the Jewish tradition into the Christian tradition, as the best way of explaining St Teresa Benedicta's growth in her love for Christ. By participating fully in the celebration of the liturgy, she anticipated much of what the Second Vatican Council would say about the full, active and conscious participation in the liturgy that allows the believer to touch and be part of the mystery that is being celebrated and the story of salvation that is unfolding.

I am sure that anyone who reads this book would welcome more of this kind of writing. Father Edmond might like to apply his knowledge and skill to a presentation of other Carmelite saints. Mary Magdalene de'Pazzi, Elizabeth of the Trinity and Titus Brandsma come readily to mind. Not wishing to be greedy, I thank the author for this present volume, and look forward to whatever might follow. May every reader be blessed with a desire to know more about the spiritual life of every believer, and the riches that we find in the saints.

Míceál O'Neill O. Carm.
Prior General, Order of the Brothers of the Blessed Virgin of Mount Carmel
Curia Generalizia dei Carmelitani, Rome
31 May 2021, Feast of the Visitation of Our Lady

Introduction

For Lent 2020 I had planned a series of 'conversations' on the writings of the Carmelite authors. The idea was to take a key passage, give some background information on the author, set the passage in the context of the work from which it was drawn, then read the passage and have a discussion on it with the participants. We had held two sessions when the public health emergency brought about by the Covid-19 pandemic meant that we had to cancel any further meetings. I therefore decided during lockdown to write up the research I had been doing on the Carmelite authors and turn it into a book.

Lectio Divina

Since what our group had been doing was a form of *Lectio Divina*, it will be useful to explain what this involves. *Lectio Divina* means sacred reading. It is usually applied to the reading of Sacred Scripture but can also be used for other spiritual writings. There are three basic movements in the traditional practice of *Lectio Divina*: *lectio, meditatio* and *oratio*.

Lectio involves reading the text and listening to it. In the ancient world, books were scarce and people read slowly and savoured the text. This kind of reading is like listening to music. One listens to music in order to *listen* to music. The same piece can be listened to over and over again. *Lectio* is reading for the sake of reading, to savour the text and really listen to it.

Meditatio is about deepening one's appreciation of the reading. It is often compared to a cow chewing the cud, digesting the reading. For an individual doing *Lectio Divina*, this might mean going back over particularly striking words or phrases and repeating them. In a group, people might share what they found interesting in the reading, what it reminded them of or what they thought about it.

Oratio means prayer. After reading the text and meditating on it, one is moved to prayer. This prayer would usually be short and spontaneous.

Many authors add a fourth movement, namely *contemplatio* or contemplation, which would be dwelling in silence on the word we have received. In the broader sense, the whole exercise is contemplative. Some authors add further elements such as *actio* or action. Prayer should influence our behaviour, and one may see discerning this as part of one's *Lectio Divina*.

The Carmelite Authors
The Carmelite authors whose writings I will discuss in this book are St Teresa of Ávila, St John of the Cross, Brother Lawrence of the Resurrection, St Thérèse of Lisieux and St Edith Stein (St Teresa Benedicta of the Cross). In each case, I have taken a significant passage from the work of each author. I am proposing these passages for *Lectio Divina*, in which the normal procedure is to take a short passage for reading, meditation and prayer. The chosen passages may also serve as introductions to the works from which they are taken.

The first two chapters are devoted to St Teresa of Ávila. Chapter One looks at her book *The Way of Perfection*. The chosen passages are Chapters 26 and 28, which deal with recollection – a concept that is central to St Teresa's teaching on prayer. Chapter Two examines her masterpiece, *The Interior Castle*. From this, I have chosen the Fourth Dwelling Places for our consideration. This part of *The Interior Castle* marks the crucial transition from ordinary prayer to the beginnings of supernatural contemplation.

In Chapter Three, we turn our attention to St John of the Cross. From his works, I have chosen *The Dark Night* which may be helpful to readers who are dealing with difficult periods in their lives. The poem 'The Dark Night' is discussed, and then from St John's commentary on the poem I have chosen Chapter 10 of Book One, which gives us his advice on how to respond to the experience of the dark night.

Our third author is Brother Lawrence of the Resurrection. Chapter Four examines *The Practice of the Presence of God*, which is a composite work comprising maxims and letters written by Brother Lawrence, and conversations with him recounted by his friend and editor, the Abbé Joseph de Beaufort. I summarise the conversations and examine some of the letters in which Brother Lawrence explains his simple but profound method of prayer.

I have devoted Chapters Five and Six to St Thérèse of Lisieux. In Chapter Five, I give an account of the members of Thérèse's family who were a major influence on her life. We look at some of the incidents in Thérèse's early life recounted in her autobiography. I also introduce the two missionaries adopted by Thérèse as her spiritual brothers. We look at her correspondence with these two men with whom Thérèse felt a special bond, and for whom she offered her prayer and suffering. Chapter Six is devoted to St Thérèse's best-known work, her autobiography *Story of a Soul.* We look at 'Manuscript B', where Thérèse tells us how she discovered her vocation to be 'love at the heart of the Church'. It is also in this part of the autobiography that Thérèse explains her 'Little Way'.

Our final author is St Edith Stein, presented in the liturgical calendar as St Teresa Benedicta of the Cross, but better known as the writer Edith Stein. From her many philosophical and theological works, I have chosen the essay 'The Prayer of the Church'. This short work gives us a remarkable insight into Edith's spirituality. It shows her understanding of the continuity between Jewish and Christian prayer and how both the liturgy and contemplative prayer are the Prayer of the Church.

Dialogue with Chiara Lubich

As our group reading the Carmelite authors grew out of a Focolare Word of Life meeting, I have tried to make connections between Carmelite spirituality and the spirituality of the Focolare Movement. This takes the form of a 'Dialogue with Chiara Lubich' with each of the authors.

CHAPTER ONE

Saint Teresa of Ávila

The Way of Perfection

Teresa de Cepeda y Ahumada was born in Ávila, Spain, in 1515, the fifth of twelve children. Teresa's mother died when she was thirteen, so her father sent her to a convent of Augustinian nuns in Ávila to be looked after and receive a basic education.

At the age of twenty, Teresa entered the Carmelite Convent of the Incarnation in Ávila. In religion she took the name Teresa of Jesus. Her early years in religious life were overshadowed by bad health. At one stage she was thought to be on the point of death and received the last rites. She remained paralysed for three years and attributed her eventual cure to the intercession of St Joseph.

It is sometimes said that life begins at forty. This was certainly true for Teresa. At thirty-nine, she had a spiritual awakening. She became unsatisfied with life at the Convent of the Incarnation. The community there was too large, and a certain worldliness had crept in. Nuns spent a lot of time entertaining their friends and relations in the parlour. The class distinction which was such a prominent feature of Spanish society at the time was reflected in life in the convent. Those who had been grand ladies before they entered the convent continued to be grand ladies in the convent and did not do household chores.

Teresa came up with the idea of returning to the original ideals of the Carmelite Order. In 1562, when she was forty-seven, she founded St Joseph's Convent in Ávila. She believed that the contemplative ideal could be better pursued in a small community. The Lord had begun with a community of twelve friends, so Teresa thought that was a good way for her to start as well. The Incarnation had a community of one hundred and eighty nuns. She also believed in strict enclosure, poverty and dedication to prayer. Everyone, including Teresa, did household chores.

Teresa went on to found sixteen more convents before her death in 1582 at the age of sixty-seven. So, although she was the great contemplative, during those twenty years from 1562 to 1582, Teresa was one of the most active people in Spain at the time. These were years spent travelling, writing and dealing with all the practical issues involved in her foundations. She had to deal with bishops, papal nuncios, provincials and other ecclesiastics, many of whom were not at all helpful, as well as with civil officials, builders and tradesmen.

Saint Teresa's Writings
Saint Teresa's first book was *The Book of Her Life*, written at the request of her spiritual director. This gives an account of her life up to the founding of St Joseph's Convent. It is really the story of her soul, as she gives an account of her experiences in prayer. *The Way of Perfection* was written at the request of her own nuns who were looking for guidance in prayer. It contains her teaching on prayer and an extended meditation on the Our Father. *The Interior Castle,* considered by many to be her masterpiece, is a systematic account of the spiritual journey. It uses the image of a castle with many rooms, with God enthroned in the innermost chamber. The castle is the soul and, as one progresses in prayer and in the

spiritual life, one gets ever closer to the inner room where God is. *The Book of Foundations* takes up the story of Teresa's life again with an account of the founding of the other convents. Teresa also wrote *Meditations on the Song of Songs* and *Spiritual Testimonies*, as well as hundreds of letters – a large body of which has survived. Saint Teresa is one of the earliest writers in Castilian Spanish. Her style is very accessible, often conversational. She addresses the reader directly. She often uses familiar objects, such as water, to explain her ideas.

Her Theology

Most great theologians construct their theology on the basis of one simple idea, as it gives unity and coherence to their thought. For Teresa, this idea is friendship. Friendship was the basic idea that she had for reforming religious life. This was why she wanted small communities, not large institutions. It was also why she wanted to overcome the class distinction of the time. She writes, 'all must be friends, all must be loved, all must be held dear, all must be helped'.[1]

Friendship was also the basic idea in Teresa's teaching on our relationship with God. Aristotle had held that friendship was not possible between God and human beings, because the disparity between the two sides was too great. Friendship had to be based on having something in common. This something in common created the possibility of sharing life and mutual giving and receiving. How could this be possible between Creator and creature? The answer, of course, is the Incarnation. God took the initiative and became a human being, sharing in our life so that we could share in God's life. Teresa maintained that the

---

[1] Saint Teresa of Ávila, *The Way of Perfection*, Chapter 4, *The Collected Works of Saint Teresa of Avila*, translated by Kieran Kavanaugh OCD and Otilio Rodriguez OCD (Washington: ICS Publications, 1980), Vol. 2, p. 55.

surest and most direct way to God was through the humanity of Christ, because this was the way that God had chosen to approach us. She saw prayer as essentially conversation with the Divine Friend.

> For mental prayer in my opinion is nothing else than an intimate sharing between friends; it means taking time to be alone with him who we know loves us.[2]

The Way of Perfection

As mentioned, St Teresa wrote *The Way of Perfection* in response to a request from her own nuns in St Joseph's for guidance on the life of prayer. She begins by explaining why she founded St Joseph's. It was so that the Lord would have some friends who would pray for the preachers and theologians and those engaged in the active mission of the Church. Its primary purpose was that the nuns would be engaged in ceaseless prayer. She wanted them to live in poverty so as to imitate the Lord's poverty and to rely on Divine Providence. She wanted a good deal of silence and solitude, because these were conducive to prayer, but she did not advocate austerity for its own sake. 'Do not think, my friends and daughters, that I shall burden you with many things.'[3] She did, however, emphasise three things which she regarded as forming an essential foundation for the life of her religious community.

---

[2] Saint Teresa of Ávila, *The Book of Her Life*, Chapter 8, *The Collected Works of Saint Teresa of Avila*, translated by Kieran Kavanaugh OCD and Otilio Rodriguez OCD (Washington: ICS Publications, 1987), Vol. 1, p. 96.
[3] Saint Teresa of Ávila, *The Way of Perfection*, Chapter 4, *The Collected Works of Saint Teresa of Avila*, translated by Kieran Kavanaugh OCD and Otilio Rodriguez OCD (Washington: ICS Publications, 1980), Vol. 2, p. 54.

> The first of these is love for one another; the second is detachment from all created things; the third is humility, which, even though I speak of it last, is the main practice and embraces all the others.[4]

Saint Teresa distinguished between vocal prayer and mental prayer. Vocal prayer is the recitation of set prayers such as the 'Our Father' or the 'Hail Mary'. Mental prayer is spontaneous prayer, when we pray in our own words or without words, usually having reflected on a truth of the faith or an incident or saying from the Gospels. Although Teresa was an advocate and teacher of mental prayer, she had a high regard for vocal prayer. The important thing was that the prayer be said with attention.

> What I would like us to do, daughters, is refuse to be satisfied with merely pronouncing the words. For when I say, 'I believe', it seems to me right that I should know and understand what I believe. And when I say, 'Our Father', it will be an act of love to understand who this Father of ours is and who the Master is who taught us this prayer.[5]

When vocal prayer is said properly it is the same as mental prayer. It is a real communication between friends. In fact, Teresa regarded the 'Our Father' as the perfect prayer.

---

[4] Saint Teresa of Ávila, *The Way of Perfection*, Chapter 4, *The Collected Works of Saint Teresa of Avila*, translated by Kieran Kavanaugh OCD and Otilio Rodriguez OCD (Washington: ICS Publications, 1980), Vol. 2, p. 54

[5] Saint Teresa of Ávila, *The Way of Perfection*, Chapter 24, *The Collected Works*, Vol. 2, p. 129.

To keep you from thinking that little is gained through a perfect recitation of vocal prayer, I tell you that it is very possible that while you are reciting the Our Father or some other vocal prayer, the Lord may raise you to perfect contemplation.[6]

What happens in this perfect contemplation is that the soul is brought beyond the noise of words. 'The soul is being enkindled in love, and it does not understand how it loves.'[7] Teresa says that in vocal and mental prayer we can do something ourselves with the help of God, but, in contemplation, it is God who does everything.

Saint Teresa's Teaching on Recollection

As I pointed out in the introduction, with each of our authors I intend to select key passages which the reader may wish to use for *Lectio Divina*. I have selected passages from *The Way of Perfection*, in which Teresa explains the practice of recollection.

In Chapter 26, Teresa says that she is addressing her remarks to those who cannot keep their minds from distraction and who find it difficult to concentrate or follow a line of thought. She says she understands this difficulty very well, because she suffered from it herself for many years.

I'm not asking you now that you think about Him or that you draw out a lot of concepts or make long and subtle reflections with your intellect. I'm not asking you to do anything more than look at Him.[8]

---

[6] Saint Teresa of Ávila, *The Way of Perfection*, Chapter 25, *The Collected Works*, Vol. 2, p. 131.

[7] Ibid.

[8] Saint Teresa of Ávila, *The Way of Perfection*, Chapter 26, *The Collected Works*, Vol. 2, pp. 133–4.

Teresa goes on to explain how the Lord accommodates himself to the person praying. She says: if you are joyful, think of him as risen; if you are sad, think of him in his sufferings in the garden. All of this suggests the use of the imagination. She says this is what a wife is expected to do: she must go along with her husband's moods. She puts in a humorous aside here: 'See what subjection you have been freed from, Sisters!'[9] In our relationship with the Lord, he actually does this for us.

She also says it may be useful to have a little picture of the Lord. What is important is to continue the conversation with God. Like any other relationship, our friendship with God depends on communication.

> Since you speak with other persons, why must words fail you when you speak with God? Don't believe they will; at least I will not believe they will if you acquire the habit. Otherwise, the failure to communicate with a person causes both estrangement and a failure to know how to speak with him ... Family ties and friendship are lost through a lack of communication.[10]

Teresa goes on to recommend the use of a good book written in the vernacular. She would undoubtedly have recommended the Gospels, but they were not available in Spanish. Teresa and her contemporaries had to make do with the so-called 'Lives' of Christ and the saints. The Holy Scriptures were only available in Latin, which, in practice, meant they were only available to the clergy. In the universities of Alcalá and Salamanca they were studied in the original Hebrew and Greek.

---

[9] Saint Teresa of Ávila, *The Way of Perfection*, Chapter 26, *The Collected Works*, Vol. 2, p. 134.
[10] Ibid., p. 136.

Teresa makes very few references to the liturgy as a source of prayer. The reason is that this too was in Latin and so was unintelligible to the people she was writing for, who were mostly religious sisters. Today, we are in a much happier position in terms of the resources available to us. We now have the scriptures in handy editions and readable translations. They can readily be used as the basis of our prayer, be that *Lectio Divina* or an Ignatian type of meditation. We not only have the Mass, but also the Liturgy of the Hours in the vernacular. Beginning our prayer with recollection, as Teresa teaches, we can proceed to take part in these vocal prayers with attention and devotion.

In Chapter 28 we get a clearer picture of what Teresa means when she says to look at the Lord. To look at the Lord is to turn one's attention inward to the presence of God in one's heart. This act of turning inwards involves shutting out what is outward.

> All one need do is go into solitude and look at Him within oneself, and not turn away from so good a Guest but with great humility speak to him as to a father.[11]

She goes on to say that by humility she does not mean faintheartedness. We should take the Lord at his word and approach him with confidence. For Teresa, humility included a certain boldness. This was in keeping with her own personality.

Saint Teresa did not teach a method of meditation in the sense of following various steps. What she did teach was the practice of recollection. If one is recollected, then one can proceed to pray, either vocally or mentally.

---

[11] Saint Teresa of Ávila, *The Way of Perfection*, Chapter 28, *The Collected Works*, Vol. 2, pp. 140–1.

This prayer is called 'recollection' because the soul collects its faculties together and enters within itself to be with its God ... Those who by such a method can enclose themselves within this little heaven of the soul, where the Maker of heaven and earth is present, and grow accustomed to refuse to be where the exterior senses in their distraction have gone or look in that direction should believe that they are following an excellent path and that they will not fail to drink water from the fount; for they will journey far in a short time.[12]

Water was one of Teresa's favourite images for prayer. The thirsty soul is refreshed with the water of contemplation and yet thirsts for more. She also uses many different images, like that of the bees going into the hive to make honey. She was really a poet, even when she wrote in prose. In Chapter 28 she also uses the image of the beautiful castle which she was to develop further in *The Interior Castle*. This will be the subject of our next chapter.

Dialogue with Chiara Lubich
Saint Teresa tells us to turn our eyes to look at Jesus. Chiara Lubich develops the same idea.

'Rejoice always' (1 Th 5:6). There is a secret, therefore, of how to remain always in joy. It consists in keeping our eyes fixed on Jesus, doing everything such that He would always shine in us. We already know the way Jesus lives in us if we strive to put His words into practice, especially if we love Him in every brother, ready to give our life for every person, as He had done.

---

[12] Saint Teresa of Ávila, *The Way of Perfection*, Chapter 28, *The Collected Works*, Vol. 2, pp. 141–2.

If our brother then loves Jesus in us, our joy will be complete (cf. Jn 15:11), because Jesus will also shine in our midst.[13]

Readings for *Lectio Divina*

The Way of Perfection, Chapter 26, paragraphs 2–3
(*Collected Works*, Volume 2, pages 133–4)

O Sisters, those of you who cannot engage in much discursive reflection with the intellect or keep your mind from distraction, get used to this practice! Get used to it! See, I know that you can do this; for I suffered many years from the trial – and it is a very great one – of not being able to quiet the mind in anything. But I know that the Lord does not leave us so abandoned; for if we humbly ask him for this friendship, He will not deny it to us. And if we cannot succeed in one year, we will succeed later. Let's not regret the time that is so well spent. Who's making us hurry? I am speaking of acquiring this habit and of striving to walk alongside this true Master.

I'm not asking you now that you think about Him or that you draw out a lot of concepts or make long and subtle reflections with the intellect. I'm not asking that you do anything more than look at Him. For who can keep you from turning the eyes of your soul toward this Lord, even if you do so just for a moment if you can't do more. You can look at very ugly things; won't you be able to look at the most beautiful thing imaginable? Well now, daughters, your Spouse never takes His eyes off you. He has suffered you committing a thousand ugly offences and abominations against Him, and this suffering wasn't enough for Him to cease looking at you. Is it too much to ask you to turn your eyes from these exterior things in order to look at Him sometimes?

---

[13] Chiara Lubich, 'Word of Life', December 1978.

Behold, He is not waiting for anything else, as He says to the bride, than that we look at Him. In the measure you desire Him, you will find Him. He so esteems our turning to look at Him that no diligence will be lacking on His part.

The Way of Perfection, Chapter 26, paragraphs 4–5 (Collected Works, Volume 2, pages 134–5)

They say that for a woman to be a good wife toward her husband she must be sad when he is sad, and joyful when he is joyful, even though she may not be so. (See what subjection you have been saved from, Sisters!) The Lord, without deception, truly acts in such a way with us. He is the one who submits, and He wants you to be the lady with authority to rule; He submits to your will. If you are joyful, look at Him as risen. Just imagining how He rose from the tomb will fill you with joy. The brilliance! The beauty! The majesty! How victorious! How joyful! Indeed, like one coming forth from a battle where he has gained a great kingdom! And all of that, plus Himself, He desires for you. Well, is it such a big thing that from time to time you turn your eyes to look upon one who gives you so much?

If you are experiencing trials or are sad, behold Him on the way to the garden: what great affliction He bore in His soul; for having become suffering itself, He tells us about it and complains of it. Or behold Him bound to the column, filled with pain, with all His flesh torn in pieces for the great love He bears you; so much suffering, persecuted by some, spit on by others, denied by His friends, abandoned by them, with no one to defend Him, frozen from the cold, left so alone that you can console each other. Or behold Him burdened by the cross, for they didn't even let Him take a breath. He will look at you with those eyes so beautiful and compassionate, filled with tears; He will forget His sorrows so as to console you in yours, merely because you yourselves go to Him to be consoled, and you turn your head to look at Him.

The Way of Perfection, Chapter 28, paragraphs 2, 4–5 (*Collected Works,* Volume 2, pages 140–2)

You already know that God is everywhere. It's obvious then, that where the king is there is his court; in sum, wherever God is, there is heaven. Without a doubt you can believe that where His Majesty is present, all glory is present. Consider what St Augustine says, that he sought Him in many places but found Him ultimately within himself. Do you think it matters little for a soul with a wandering mind to understand this truth and see that there is no need to go to heaven in order to speak with one's Eternal Father or find delight in Him? Nor is there any need to shout. However softly we speak, He is near enough to hear us. Neither is there any need for wings to go to find Him. All one need do is go into solitude and look at Him within oneself, and not turn away from so good a Guest but with great humility speak to Him as a father. Beseech Him as you would a father; tell Him about your trials; ask Him for a remedy against them, realising that you are not worthy to be His daughter.

The intellect is recollected much more quickly with this kind of prayer even though it may be vocal; it is a prayer that brings with it many blessings. This prayer is called 'recollection', because the soul collects its faculties together and enters within itself to be with its God. And its divine Master comes more quickly to teach it and give it the prayer of quiet than He would through any other method it might use. For centred there within itself, it can think about the Passion and represent the Son and offer Him to the Father and not tire the intellect by going to look for Him on Mount Calvary or in the garden or the pillar.

Those who by such a method can enclose themselves within this little heaven of our soul, where the Master of heaven and earth is present, and grow accustomed to refusing to be where the exterior senses in their distraction have gone or look in that direction should believe they are following an excellent path and that they will not fail to drink water from the fount; for they will journey far in a short time. Their situation is like that of a person who travels by ship; with a little wind he reaches the end of his journey in a few days. But those who go by land take longer.

CHAPTER TWO

Saint Teresa of Ávila

The Interior Castle

In *The Book of Her Life* which Teresa completed in 1565, she gives an account of her experiences in prayer. In May 1577, she was discussing some of the contents with her confessor and friend Fr Gratian, and lamenting the fact that the manuscript had been given to the Inquisition and it was not clear whether she would ever get it back. The Inquisition was very suspicious of people who claimed to have had mystical experiences and, particularly, of women mystics. Father Gratian suggested that she write another book, giving an account of the development of her prayer life, but describing it in general terms without claiming that she had experienced any of it herself. This seemed like a good way of making her doctrine available and, at the same time, avoiding the censure of the Inquisition. So, Gratian 'ordered' her to write the book. The result was *The Dwelling Places* or, as it is better known, *The Interior Castle*. Teresa completed it by the end of November 1577, despite the fact that this was a very difficult year for her. The Carmelite provincial was against her and the papal nuncio, who had been her supporter, died. As a result, the future of her whole project of reform was in question. She wrote mostly during periods of prayer and it probably helped her to put aside for a while the various problems that beset her. It is characterised by serenity and the wisdom of mature reflection.

As with *The Way of Perfection,* I do not intend to examine the whole of *The Interior Castle,* but to take one section from which we may take passages to be used for *Lectio Divina.* This will be taken from the Fourth Dwelling Places. Nevertheless, some general remarks will be helpful. Teresa begins by proposing an image which will provide the basis for her reflections.

> It is that we consider our soul to be like a castle made entirely out of diamond or of very clear crystal, in which there are many rooms, just as in heaven there are many dwelling places.[1]

The first thing that is remarkable is the very positive view of the human being that Teresa has; this could be termed her anthropology. The soul is beautiful because it is made in the image of God.

> I don't find anything comparable to the magnificent beauty of a soul and its marvellous capacity. Indeed, our intellects, however keen, can hardly comprehend it, just as they cannot comprehend God; but He Himself says that He created us in His own image and likeness.[2]

There are seven dwelling places or sets of dwelling places (Teresa uses the plural) in the castle and the book is structured accordingly, beginning with the First Dwelling Places, and proceeding inwards to the Seventh Dwelling Places, which are in the deepest centre of the castle. Here God is enthroned, giving

---

[1] Saint Teresa of Ávila, *The Interior Castle,* First Dwellings, Chapter 1, *The Collected Works of Saint Teresa of Avila,* translated by Kieran Kavanaugh OCD and Otilio Rodriguez OCD, Vol. 2, p. 283.
[2] Ibid.

light to the whole crystal structure. In each of the dwelling places (in modern parlance we might call them 'apartments') there are rooms in which God communicates with the soul and bestows favours upon it. Just as the soul in a state of grace is like this beautiful crystal palace all lit up and sparkling, so the soul in mortal sin is like the castle with the lights turned off and is like a black lump of coal, although God is still present, keeping it in existence.

In *The Interior Castle*, St Teresa envisages the spiritual life as a journey inwards through the various apartments and rooms, growing in intimacy with God who is at the centre. The castle is entered through prayer.

> Insofar as I can understand, the gate of entry to this castle is prayer and reflection. I don't mean to refer to mental more than vocal prayer, for since vocal prayer is prayer it must be accompanied by reflection.[3]

Lest readers think that prayer can be engaged in apart from the normal demands of the Christian life, Teresa is very clear about the basics.

> Let us understand, my daughters, that true perfection consists in love of God and neighbour; the more perfectly we keep these two commandments, the more perfect we will be.[4]

In the first three Dwelling Places, Teresa describes the development of one's prayer life and at the same time

---

[3] Saint Teresa of Ávila, *The Interior Castle*, First Dwellings, Chapter 1, *The Collected Works of Saint Teresa of Avila*, translated by Kieran Kavanaugh OCD and Otilio Rodriguez OCD, Vol. 2, p. 286.

[4] Saint Teresa of Ávila, *The Interior Castle*, First Dwellings, Chapter 2, *The Collected Works of Saint Teresa of Avila*, Vol. 2, pp. 295–6.

one's growth in virtue. These two are always linked in her thought. Prayer being the expression of one's relationship with God, it cannot progress if it is contradicted by the rest of one's life. The test of the authenticity of one's prayer is not whether one experiences consolation, but whether one is doing God's will in one's everyday life.

> The whole aim of any person who is beginning prayer – and don't forget this, because it's very important – should be that he work and prepare himself with determination and every possible effort to bring his will into conformity with God's will.[5]

Teresa wants to demystify the whole enterprise of contemplative prayer and Christian perfection. For her it is quite simply about doing God's will.

> Don't think that in what concerns perfection there is some mystery or things unknown or still to be understood, for in perfect conformity to God's will lies all our good.[6]

Even though the formula for perfection is simple, it is also demanding. So, Teresa stresses the need for perseverance. One must not become discouraged in the face of dryness in prayer and in having to become detached from earthly riches and honours. In the Third Dwelling Places, Teresa discusses the traditional virtue of 'fear of the Lord' which is mainly about the avoidance of sin.

In the Fourth Dwelling Places, Teresa explains the transition from the kind of recollected prayer that we

---

[5] Saint Teresa of Ávila, *The Interior Castle*, Second Dwellings, Chapter 1, *The Collected Works of Saint Teresa of Avila*, Vol. 2, p. 301.
[6] Ibid.

can make by our own efforts with God's help to a deeper kind of recollection which is given by God and which leads to the prayer of quiet. This is the beginning of the kind of prayer that Teresa calls 'supernatural' because it does not depend on our own efforts, but on the action of God. Other authors call it 'mystical contemplation' or 'infused contemplation'. We will return to these Dwelling Places, having briefly surveyed the remaining three Dwelling Places.

In the Fifth Dwelling Places, Teresa explains the prayer of union. The soul briefly experiences being absorbed in God. Afterwards, the soul has certainty that it has experienced union with God. Teresa again stresses the importance of doing God's will.

> True union can very well be reached, with God's help, if we make the effort to obtain it by keeping our wills fixed on that which is only God's will.[7]

God asks of us love of God and of our neighbour. Loving our neighbour is the surest sign that we love God. In the Fifth Dwelling Places, Teresa introduces the marriage symbolism which she will develop further in the remaining Dwelling Places.

In the Sixth Dwelling Places, which is the longest section of *The Interior Castle*, containing eleven chapters, Teresa deals with locutions, visions and ecstasies. She also deals with the kind of suffering a soul may go through. She advises her readers not to get lost in an abstract idea of the Divinity, but to dwell on the humanity and divinity of Christ. Jesus is always the Way.

In the Seventh Dwelling Places, the soul arrives at a new kind of union with God. There is a peace and

---

[7] Saint Teresa of Ávila, *The Interior Castle*, Fifth Dwellings, Chapter 3, *The Collected Works of Saint Teresa of Avila*, Vol. 2, p. 349.

tranquillity that pervades one's whole life. There is no doubt that Teresa herself experienced this and that was why she did not lose her serenity in the midst of all the external difficulties she was experiencing while writing this book. Often in *The Interior Castle*, Teresa introduces what she is about to describe by saying: 'I know a person who had this experience.' It is obvious that the person is herself. In the Seventh Dwelling Places she describes the experience of spiritual marriage.

> The Lord represented Himself to her, just after she had received Communion, in the form of shining splendour, beauty, and majesty, as He was after His resurrection, and He told her that now it was time that she consider as her own what belonged to Him and that He would take care of what was hers.[8]

The Fourth Dwelling Places: The Prayer of Quiet
There are three chapters in the Fourth Dwelling Places. Saint Teresa begins by describing the consolation and joy one sometimes experiences during meditation. These feelings are natural and, to some extent, depend on our temperament.

> They are to be esteemed if there is the humility to understand that one is no better because of experiencing them, for it cannot be known whether they are all effects of love.[9]

---

[8] Saint Teresa of Ávila, *The Interior Castle*, Seventh Dwellings, Chapter 2, *The Collected Works of Saint Teresa of Avila*, Vol. 2, pp. 432–3.
[9] Saint Teresa of Ávila, *The Interior Castle*, Fourth Dwellings, Chapter 1, *The Collected Works of Saint Teresa of Avila*, Vol. 2, pp. 318–9.

These devout feelings are good, but if one can make acts of love that is better.

> I only wish to inform you that in order to profit by this path and ascend to the dwelling places we desire, the important thing is not to think much but to love much; and so do that which best stirs you to love.[10]

Teresa herself found it impossible to follow the kind of discursive reasoning which many books on meditation proposed at the time. She tells us that when she discovered the distinction between the mind and the intellect, she found this very helpful. The mind flies about, but this does not impede the intellect from being focused on God. In other words, if our inner self is focused on God and directing our attention to prayer, it does not matter if thoughts and images come and go in our minds. It is best to pay them no attention.

> Just as we cannot stop the movement of the heavens, but they proceed in rapid motion, so neither can we stop our mind ... But the soul is perhaps completely joined with Him in the dwelling places very close to the centre while the mind is on the outskirts of the castle suffering from a thousand wild and poisonous beasts ... As a result we should not be disturbed; nor should we abandon prayer, which is what the devil wants us to do.[11]

Having described the natural consolations that arise during prayer, Teresa goes on in Chapter 2 to contrast

---

[10] Saint Teresa of Ávila, *The Interior Castle*, Fourth Dwellings, Chapter 1, *The Collected Works of Saint Teresa of Avila*, Vol. 2, p. 319.
[11] Ibid., p. 320.

these with what she calls 'spiritual delights'. These come from God and so, have a supernatural source. This is the prayer of quiet. In both cases the soul is recollected, but one is worked at, whereas the other is given by God. Teresa explains this with the image of the two water troughs being filled.

> These two troughs are filled with water in different ways; with one the water comes from far away through many aqueducts and the use of much ingenuity; with the other the source of the water is right there, and the trough fills without any noise.[12]

The water coming through the aqueducts stands for the natural consolations. The spring bubbling up within the trough stands for the spiritual delights. There is no effort involved.

> With this other fount, the water comes from its own source, which is God. And since His Majesty desires to do so – when He is pleased to grant some supernatural favour – He produces this delight with the greatest peace and quiet and sweetness in the very interior part of ourselves ... this water overflows through all the dwelling places and faculties until reaching the body.[13]

The effects of this prayer completely surpass the consolations of the former. They even overflow into the body. There is no dualism in Teresa's concept of the human being, even though she again speaks of the beauty of the soul. Contemplative prayer is a gift from God, but it comes from within the depths of the

---

[12] Saint Teresa of Ávila, *The Interior Castle,* Fourth Dwellings, Chapter 2, *The Collected Works of Saint Teresa of Avila,* Vol. 2, p. 323.
[13] Ibid., p. 324.

human soul, because that is where God is present. One is reminded of the words of Our Lord to the Samaritan woman: 'The water that I will give will become in them a spring of water gushing up to eternal life' (Jn 4:14).

Teresa goes on to tell her readers that they do well to desire this prayer and she says they will want to know how it can be obtained. The only way is through humility.

> After you have done what should be done in the previous dwelling places: humility! humility! By this means the Lord allows Himself to be conquered with regard to anything we want from Him.[14]

Humility includes the sense that we do not deserve these favours. Teresa goes on to say that the prayer of quiet is received without seeking it or striving for it. This is because it depends on God's action, not ours.

While the prayer of quiet cannot be reached by our own efforts, we can make ourselves available for it, so to speak. We can practise recollection. Teresa explained this in *The Way of Perfection*. Here, in Chapter 3 of the Fourth Dwelling Places, she explains that we can be brought into a deeper kind of recollection by the Lord. She uses the beautiful image of the shepherd's whistle.

> Like a good shepherd, with a whistle so gentle that even they themselves almost fail to hear it, He makes them recognise His voice and stops them from going so far astray and brings them back to their dwelling place.[15]

---

[14] Saint Teresa of Ávila, *The Interior Castle*, Fourth Dwellings, Chapter 2, *The Collected Works of Saint Teresa of Avila*, Vol. 2, p. 326.
[15] Saint Teresa of Ávila, *The Interior Castle*, Fourth Dwellings, Chapter 3, *The Collected Works of Saint Teresa of Avila*, Vol. 2, p. 328.

Again, one is reminded of words from the Fourth Gospel: 'My sheep hear my voice. I know them, and they follow me' (Jn 10:27).

Teresa also uses the image of the hedgehog curling up, which is the recollection we ourselves do, but points out that what she is describing is not quite the same because it is passive.

> One noticeably senses a gentle drawing inward, as anyone who goes through this will observe ... I have read where it was compared to a hedgehog curling up or a turtle drawing into its shell ... But these creatures draw inward whenever they want. In the case of this recollection, it does not come when we want it but when God wants to grant us the favour.[16]

God grants the favour to persons who are already becoming detached from material things. Teresa makes the point that married people do so in desire not in deed, as their state of life requires them to deal with the things of the world. Although she was writing mainly for her own nuns, Teresa clearly regarded contemplative prayer as open to everyone.

In the rest of Chapter 3, Teresa counsels against false notions of contemplative prayer and again stresses the need to avoid sin and to persevere in prayer. In particular, she advises against trying to stop the mind from thinking. The effort to do so causes more harm than good. The recollection that is given by the Lord's action and the prayer of quiet that follows from it are always peaceful and gentle. They cannot be forced.

Teresa says that we can be sure we are on the right path if the prayer produces the effect of making us

---

[16] Saint Teresa of Ávila, *The Interior Castle*, Fourth Dwellings, Chapter 3, *The Collected Works of Saint Teresa of Avila*, Vol. 2, p. 328.

grow in love. Genuine growth in prayer produces an improvement in all the virtues. It creates a kind of expansion of the heart, so that we are motivated more by love than by fear and experience freedom of spirit. Sometimes sisters go into a kind of stupor and think that this is contemplative prayer. In this situation, Teresa advises that the sister should cut down on the amount of time spent in prayer; the prioress should make sure that she gets enough sleep and proper food and that the sister be given active tasks to keep her busy. Otherwise the sister's health will deteriorate.

Dialogue with Chiara Lubich

There are many similarities between St Teresa and Chiara Lubich. Both started movements of spirituality and made a significant contribution to the life of the Church. Both left behind writings that are of great theological and spiritual value. I think Teresa would have recognised Chiara as a kindred spirit. Chiara admired Teresa; the Focolare Movement has a shared spirituality. Chiara saw the need for a communal spirituality, of going to God together. She believed that in our day, St Teresa's image of the 'interior castle' needs to be complemented by the image of the 'exterior castle'.

Saint Teresa of Ávila, a doctor of the church, speaks of an 'interior castle'. It is the soul with the divine dwelling at the centre, revealing and shedding light on everything throughout life, allowing it to overcome every sort of trial. Even though St Teresa drew all her daughters into this experience, it is a height of sanctity that is primarily personal.

But then came the moment at least so it seemed to us, of discovery, of shedding light upon and building not just the 'interior castle' but the 'exterior castle'.

We see the whole movement as an exterior castle, where Christ is present, illuminating every part of it from the centre to the periphery.[17]

Just as St Teresa saw the castle as an image of the beauty of the soul, Chiara Lubich extended the same image outwards, with Christ still at the centre, to show the beauty of the Focolare Movement which is a microcosm of the Church, the Body of Christ.

Readings for *Lectio Divina*

The Interior Castle, Fourth Dwelling Places, Chapter 2, paragraphs 3–4
(*Collected Works,* Volume 2, pages 323–4)

These two troughs are filled with water in different ways; with one the water comes from far away with many aqueducts and the use of much ingenuity; with the other the source of the water is right there, and the trough fills without any noise. If the spring is abundant, as is this one we are speaking about, the water overflows once the trough is filled, forming a large stream. There is no need of any skill, nor does the building of aqueducts have to continue; but water is always flowing from the spring.

The water coming from the aqueducts is comparable, in my opinion, to the consolations I mentioned that are drawn from meditation. For we obtain them through thoughts, assisting ourselves, using creatures to help our meditation, and tiring the intellect. Since, in the end, the consolation comes

---

[17] Chiara Lubich, *Essential Writings,* compiled and edited by Michel Vandeleene (London: New City, 2007), pp. 31–2.

from our own efforts, noise is made when there has to be some replenishing of the benefits the consolation causes in the soul, as has been said.

With the other fount, the water comes from its own source, which is God. And since His Majesty desires to do so – when He is pleased to grant some supernatural favour – He produces this delight with the greatest peace and quiet and sweetness in the very interior part of ourselves. I don't know from where or how, nor is that happiness and delight experienced as are earthly consolations in the heart. I mean there is no similarity at the beginning, for afterwards the delight fills everything; this water overflows through all the dwelling places and faculties until reaching the body. That is why I said that it begins in God and ends in ourselves. For, certainly, as anyone who may have experienced it may see, the whole exterior man enjoys this spiritual delight and sweetness.

The Interior Castle, Fourth Dwelling Places, Chapter 2, paragraphs 5–6
(*Collected Works,* Volume 2, pages 324–5)

I was now thinking, while writing this, that the verse, mentioned above, *Dilitasti cor meum,* says the heart was expanded. I don't think the experience is something, as I say, that rises from the heart, but from another part still more interior, as from something deep. I think this must be the centre of the soul, as I later came to understand and will mention at the end. For certainly I see secrets within ourselves that have often caused me to marvel. And how many more there must be! O my Lord and my God, how great are Your grandeurs! We go about here below like foolish little shepherds, for while it seems that we are getting some knowledge of You it must amount to no more than nothing; for even in our own selves there are great secrets that we don't understand. I say 'no more than nothing' because I'm comparing it to the many,

many secrets that are in You, not because the grandeurs we see in You are not extraordinary; and that includes those we can attain knowledge of through Your works.

To return to the verse, what I think is helpful in it for explaining this matter is the idea of expansion. It seems that since that heavenly water begins to rise from this spring I'm mentioning that is deep within us, it swells and expands our whole interior being producing ineffable blessings; nor does the soul even understand what is given to it there. It perceives a fragrance, let us say for now, as though there were in that interior depth a brazier giving off sweet-smelling perfumes. No light is seen, nor is the place seen where the brazier is; but the warmth and the fragrant fumes spread through the entire soul and even often enough, as I have said, the body shares in them. See now that you understand me; no heat is felt, nor is there the scent of any perfume, for the experience is more delicate than an experience of these things; but I use the examples only so as to explain it to you. And let persons who have not experienced these things understand that truthfully they do happen and are felt in this way, and the soul understands them in a manner clearer than is my explanation right now. This spiritual delight is not something that can be imagined, because however diligent our efforts we cannot acquire it. The very experience of it makes us realise that it is not of the same metal as we ourselves but fashioned from the purest gold of the divine wisdom. Here, in my opinion, the faculties are not united but absorbed and looking as though in wonder at what they see.

The Interior Castle, Fourth Dwelling Places, Chapter 3, paragraphs 1–2
(*Collected Works*, Volume 2, pages 327–8)

The effects of this prayer are many. I shall mention some. But first, I want to mention another kind of prayer that almost always begins before this one. Since I have spoken of this prayer elsewhere, I shall say little. It is a recollection that also seems to me to be supernatural because it doesn't involve being in the dark or closing the eyes, nor does it consist in any exterior thing, since without first wanting to do so, one does close one's eyes and desire solitude. It seems that without any contrivance the edifice is being built, by means of this recollection, for the prayer that was mentioned. The senses and exterior things seem to be losing their hold because the soul is recovering what it had lost.

They say that the soul enters within itself and, at other times, that it rises above itself. With such terminology I wouldn't know how to clarify anything. That's what is wrong with me: that I think you will understand by my way of explaining, while perhaps I'm the only one who will understand myself. Let us suppose that these senses and faculties (for I have already mentioned that these powers are the people of the castle, which is the image I have taken for my explanation) have gone outside and have walked for days and years with strangers – enemies of the well-being of the castle. Having seen their perdition, they have already begun to approach the castle even though they may not manage to remain inside because the habit of doing so is difficult to acquire. But still they are not traitors, and they walk in the environs of the castle. Once the great King, who is in the centre dwelling place of this castle, sees their good will, He desires in His wonderful mercy to bring them back to him. Like a good shepherd, with a whistle so gentle that even they themselves almost fail to hear it, He makes them recognise His voice and stops them from going so far astray and brings them back to their dwelling place. And this shepherd's whistle has such power that they abandon the exterior things in which they were estranged from Him and enter the castle.

CHAPTER THREE

Saint John of the Cross

The Dark Night

Juan de Yepes, known to history as St John of the Cross, was born in Fontiveros, Spain, in 1542. His father, Gonzalo de Yepes, came from a well-to-do family but was disinherited when he married Catalina Alvarez, a poor weaver. The family had three boys, one of whom died in childhood. When John was two years old, his father died. His mother Catalina moved with her two boys to the market town of Medina del Campo. John got an elementary education at a school for poor children run by the Jesuits. He helped in the sacristy and in the local hospital where he was quite good at nursing the sick. The chaplain at the hospital also encouraged him to study and taught him Latin and Greek.

At the age of twenty-one, John joined the Carmelites and took the religious name of John of St Matthias. He was sent to Salamanca for his studies. This was one the great centres of learning in Europe at the time. John was ordained into the priesthood in 1567. Around this time, he felt drawn to a more contemplative way of life than that being practised by the Carmelite friars at the time. He was considering moving to the Carthusians, but then one of those providential meetings, that sometimes happen in life, took place. John had gone to Medina del Campo to celebrate his first Mass. Saint Teresa of Ávila, or Mother Teresa of Jesus as she was known in her lifetime, happened to be there as well, having founded her second convent there. She had heard about John and asked that he come to see her. John decided to discuss his problem with her. Her response was to invite him to join her movement of reform within the Carmelite Order and do for the men what she had been doing for the women. He was immediately taken by the idea and became the first male member of Teresa's reform movement.

In November 1568, with two others, John of St Matthias renewed his religious profession as a friar of the reform, embracing the ancient Carmelite Rule and taking the name John of the Cross. He was made novice master for the small new group and they immediately started recruiting novices. By 1571, they had set up a house of studies on the outskirts of Alcalá, with John as rector. In 1572, John of the Cross was sent to Ávila where Teresa had become prioress of her old Convent of the Incarnation. He became spiritual director to the nuns, including Teresa herself, even though he was twenty-seven years her junior.

The reform movement created tensions within the Carmelite Order. Not everyone approved of Mother Teresa or her ideas. John of the Cross was captured and brought off to Toledo where he was imprisoned. Teresa did not know where he was and wrote letters to all the people she thought could help find him, including the King of Spain. In those days, many religious houses had punishment cells to deal with some of the more recalcitrant brethren. John was put in a dungeon where he spent nine months in terrible conditions. During this time, he kept sane by remembering the beauty of the Castilian countryside and by writing poetry. Eventually, having been moved from the dungeon to a cell in a tower with a more sympathetic jailer, he was able to escape with the help of a rope made from pieces of cloth. John managed to find his way to the convent that Teresa had founded in Toledo, where the nuns kept him in hiding.

When it was safe to move, John travelled to Andalusia in the far south of Spain. He took up residence in El Calvario in the Sierra del Segura. While there, he ministered to the nuns in Beas and founded a college in Baeza. John was to spend a number of years in the south. He was prior of the community in Granada from 1582 to 1588. These were places of great natural beauty. Like St Francis of Assisi, John of the Cross was very aware of the presence of God in nature and found the beauty of the countryside conducive to contemplation. He also liked to work with his hands. In Granada, John helped to build the new monastery and aqueduct himself. During those years he also travelled around founding new communities. He preached and heard confessions. He gave spiritual direction to nuns, friars and many lay people who sought him out for his advice. His prose works were written as part of this ministry. John's final posting was to the remote monastery of La Peñuela. He died in Ubeda on 14 December 1591.

Writings of St John of the Cross

Saint John of the Cross was essentially a poet. He is recognised as one of the greatest poets in the Castilian Spanish language. His prose works are mainly commentaries on his poems. He may have written some poetry before his imprisonment in Toledo, but it was during this dark period that his creative work really began. While in prison he wrote 'The Spiritual Canticle', 'For I Know Well the Spring', the Romance on the Gospel text 'In principio erat Verbum', and the poem on the psalm 'Super flumina Babylonis'. The poem 'The Dark Night' may also have been conceived in prison and written in El Calvario.

Just as St Teresa pictures the spiritual journey in terms of going ever deeper into the Interior Castle, John of the Cross used the image of climbing a mountain. *The Ascent of Mount Carmel* is a systematic treatise on the spiritual life. His prose works *The Dark Night* and *The Spiritual Canticle* are commentaries on the poems. Much of this writing was done when he was prior in Granada. His last work, *The Living Flame of Love*, is a book containing a poem with commentary. It was written for Doña Ana de Peñalosa, a friend and benefactor of the discalced friars. In his ministry of spiritual direction, especially to the nuns, John often wrote little notes with maxims or pieces of advice for his clients. Sometimes he also gave notes to the community. This is the origin of *The Sayings of Light and Love* and *The Special Counsels*.

'The Dark Night'

The poem 'The Dark Night' can be appreciated on its own without reference to the commentary that was written later. A poem has a life of its own and often the reader will find meaning in it that the author did not foresee. The poem flows directly from John's experience. In the commentary he uses the poem as a springboard to explain aspects of what people experience on the spiritual journey. Here is the first stanza.

> One dark night,
> Fired with love's urgent longings
> – Ah, the sheer grace! –
> I went out unseen,
> my house being now all stilled.[1]

---

[1] Saint John of the Cross, *The Dark Night* in *The Collected Works of St John of the Cross*, translated by Kieran Kavanaugh OCD and Otilio Rodriguez OCD (Washington: ICS Publications, 1991), p. 358.

Clearly 'The Dark Night' is a love poem. It describes the Beloved going out at night and searching for her Lover. She is guided only by the flame of love in her heart. The night is lovely because it unites the Beloved with her Lover. The last part of the poem describes them resting together under the trees. It culminates in complete forgetfulness of self.

If one were to come across this poem without ever having heard of St John of the Cross or his mystical theology, one would presume that it was simply a poem about human love, describing the passionate longing of one human being for another. The poem can be read in that way. For John, however, the Lover is God and the one searching for him is the soul, which he thinks of as feminine, even when it is a man's soul that is meant. The poem, in fact, describes John's own experience of searching for God and being united with him. The poem itself speaks of the night in positive terms.

> O guiding night!
> O night more lovely than the dawn!
> O night that has united
> the Lover with his beloved,
> transforming the beloved in her Lover.[2]

We do not get any hint that the night is a metaphor for what John calls purgation, that is the sense of privation, loss and disorientation that he describes in the commentary that follows.

The book of the Bible that seemed to resonate particularly with John's experience was the Song of Songs. He asked for it to be read when he was dying. We can see its influence here. Song of Songs 3:1-5 describes the Bride going out at night searching the

---

[2] Saint John of the Cross, *The Dark Night*, in Kavanaugh and Rodriguez, *op. cit.*, p. 359.

streets of Jerusalem for her Beloved. Song of Songs 4:12-15 describes the garden with its beautiful fragrances. John would have been familiar with the allegorical interpretation of the Song of Songs. In his day it was usually read as being about the love between Christ and his bride the Church, or as being about the relationship between God and the soul.

The Experience of the Dark Night
The expression 'the dark night of the soul' has become well known and it is often used by people when they are going through a difficult time in life. For John of the Cross, the dark night is a paradox. On the one hand it expresses the idea of privation and loss. It expresses suffering and emptiness. On the other hand, it is in this darkness that God is present. One could even say that God's presence is discerned in the experience of God's absence. The absence of God is something that can only be experienced by someone who has experienced the presence of God. This is expressed well by the English poet Elizabeth Jennings in her poem 'Absence'. She describes going into a garden which she had previously visited with the person to whom the poem is addressed. Everything is the same as it was on that occasion, except that now she is alone. She says:

> It was because the place was just the same
> That made your absence such a savage force.[3]

In a paradoxical way, if something is absent, it means it exists. This is often how the mystics experience God. It is 'the dry weary land without water' (Ps 63:1). In fact, John says that the night is beautiful, more beautiful than the dawn.

---

[3] Rebecca Watts, ed., *New Selected Poems: Elizabeth Jennings* (Manchester: Carcanet Press, 2019).

John of the Cross distinguishes between two dark nights, or two phases in the dark night. The first is the night of sense. This is when one is deprived of feelings of consolation. One has no feelings of devotion, but still one perseveres in prayer. One's faith is, in fact, becoming stronger because it is no longer reliant on having nice feelings. There is just God and faith.

The second phase is the night of spirit. Here, not only have the feelings of devotion disappeared, but God and faith seem to have disappeared as well. One is afraid that one has become an atheist. There seems to be nothing and yet one carries on. Saint Thérèse of Lisieux went through this trial.

The Dark Night, Books One and Two

The poem 'The Dark Night' consists of eight stanzas. It is followed by a commentary in two books. The commentary does not cover all eight stanzas. John comments in detail and at length on the first two stanzas, and then, briefly, on the third stanza. Book One is a treatise on the night of the senses. Book Two is a treatise on the dark night of the spirit. The passage I propose for *Lectio Divina* is Chapter 10 of Book One. It will be useful to get an overview of Book One.

In Book One, St John of the Cross is writing for those people who have been taking prayer seriously and practising meditation. He says that at the beginning, God treats the soul like a loving mother who carries her child in her arms, caressing it and feeding it. But then, at a certain stage, it becomes necessary that the mother put the child down so that it can learn to walk and do things for itself. In a similar way, at the beginning of the spiritual journey, God caresses the soul with consolations and feelings of devotion, but at a certain stage he withdraws these, so that the person may seek God himself rather than the consolations. It is easy to fall into the temptation of performing religious exercises such as prayer, fasting and the reception of the sacraments for the satisfaction that they bring, rather than to please God. In this way, what appears to be spiritual is actually carnal.

Feelings of devotion and even religious experiences, such as ecstasy, are not in themselves indications of holiness. Saint John of the Cross says that they may even be produced by the devil in order to deceive people into believing they are holy. For John, embracing the will of God is the only path to holiness. The path of aridity, which is the dark night, is a safer and surer way than following what gives satisfaction. God brings people into the dark night in order to free them from attachment to what gives satisfaction at the level of the feelings and senses. The dark night enables them to grow and find God in poverty of spirit.

The dark night has begun when a person no longer finds satisfaction in spiritual exercises. People in the dark night are no longer able to concentrate on meditation or work up feelings of devotion. This is a state of spiritual aridity. John says that there is a difference between aridity and lukewarmness. Those who have become lukewarm have lost interest in the things of God. They no longer find satisfaction in religion, but they are finding it in worldly pursuits. The person in the dark night is not finding satisfaction in anything. Those in the dark night are still very concerned to serve God and it troubles them that they do not find devotion in religious exercises as they formerly did. They are seeking God more even though they seem to be getting nothing in return. There is no feedback, so to speak.

It should also be noted that the dark night is not the same as depression – what John would have termed *melancholia*. Those who are depressed are not able to get on with their lives. Depression has a negative impact on their work and relationships. Those going through the dark night are able to continue with their normal duties and commitments.

In fact, they become more assiduous in the things of God, despite the affliction they are suffering.

The Dark Night, Book One, Chapter 10

In Chapter 10 of Book One, St John of the Cross gives advice on how people should handle this experience of the dark night. He says that most of the suffering that souls endure is not due to the experience itself, but to their reaction to it. They do not understand what is going on and so they feel they have gone wrong and must try harder to meditate or work up feelings of devotion. Not only is this to no avail, but it is actually harmful. John's advice is simply to let the process happen and be at peace. God is at work in a hidden way.

> All that is required of them here is freedom of soul, that they liberate themselves from the impediment and fatigue of ideas and thoughts, and care not about thinking and meditating. They must be content simply with a loving and peaceful attentiveness to God, and live without the concern, without the effort and without the desire to taste or feel him.[4]

The fact is that this contemplation that the person is now experiencing is passive. It is also obscure, in the sense that much is happening below the level of consciousness. God is communicating himself at a deep level.

> For contemplation is nothing else than a secret and peaceful and loving inflow of God, which, if not hampered, fires the soul in the spirit of love.[5]

---

[4] Saint John of the Cross, *The Dark Night*, in Kavanaugh and Rodriguez, *op. cit.*, p. 382.
[5] Ibid.

The person is growing in the love of God simply by attentiveness and trying to do God's will in the circumstances of everyday life. John goes on to explain that this fire of love gradually increases until one becomes aware of being drawn by God's love and filled with love for God. The dark night has produced humility and leads to a new appreciation and love for other people.

Saint John of the Cross says that the night of the senses is a common experience, whereas the night of the spirit is rare. It is when people are going about their religious exercises with delight and satisfaction that the night comes, and they are confused and disorientated. John says it is not possible to say how long the night of sense lasts.

> Those who have more considerable capacity for suffering, God purges more intensely and quickly. But those who are very weak he keeps in this night for a long time.[6]

He also says that for some people the experience of the dark night is discontinuous, in the sense that they alternate between periods of spiritual dryness and spiritual satisfaction. However, the good news is that the experience of the night does eventually give way to a new state of calm where there is spiritual satisfaction of a more gentle and quiet kind.

> In this new state, as one liberated from a cramped prison cell, it [the soul] goes about the things of God with much more freedom and satisfaction of spirit and with more abundant interior delight than it did in the beginning before entering the night of sense ... The soul

---

[6] Saint John of the Cross, *The Dark Night*, in Kavanaugh and Rodriguez, *op. cit.*, p. 394.

readily finds in its spirit, without the work of meditation, a very serene, loving contemplation and spiritual delight.[7]

This positive state of affairs will usually go on for many years. John warns, however, that the purgation of the soul is not complete. For this reason, there will be occasional bouts of aridity. For some, there will be the experience of the night of the spirit, which John says is 'frightful' and which he describes in Book Two.

Applying the Teaching

The teaching of St John of the Cross can be applied to any crisis in life. The dark night is a crisis in the spiritual life. His advice is that one will get through it by persevering in the practice of virtue and allowing God to do his work in the soul. What this means in practise is that one keeps doing one's duty, continues to pray and goes with the flow of what is happening at a psychological level. A time of crisis is a time to steer a steady course and not to make any life-changing decisions. This applies to such situations as bereavement, a mid-life crisis, job loss or a relationship breakdown.

For the person whose basic outlook in life is religious, the crisis will very often take the form of a religious crisis such as John describes. The liturgy of the Church, both the Mass and the Liturgy of the Hours, can be very helpful to the person who finds it hard to pray, because it offers an objective structure that is not dependent on one's feelings and moods.

Saint John of the Cross is also very relevant in his distrust of religious feelings and paranormal phenomena. He basically sees them as irrelevant. They are no indication of holiness. People who have

---

[7] Saint John of the Cross, *The Dark Night*, in Kavanaugh and Rodriguez, *op. cit.*, p. 395.

had an evangelical-type experience (having 'found the Lord') and are on an emotional high would be advised by John that the high will inevitably be followed by a low.

Dialogue with Chiara Lubich
Chiara Lubich saw the sense of abandonment that Jesus experienced on the cross as a kind of dark night.

> In the Bible we read of a culminating moment of suffering that is expressed in a 'Why' cried out to heaven ... And finally, that unexpected cry, 'Why have you forsaken me?' that allows us a glimpse into the drama lived by the God-Man. It is the culminating point of his sufferings, his inner passion, his darkest night. He who had said: 'The Father and I are one' lives the tragic experience of disunity, of separation from God.[8]

By identifying with those separated from God, Jesus has reached out to all and has made it possible for all humanity to be brought back to God. 'When I am lifted up from the earth, I shall draw all people to myself' (Jn 12:32). Chiara Lubich says:

> In his forsakenness, the last and greatest sign of his love, Christ reaches the point of total annihilation of self. He reopens the path to unity for all persons with God and with one another.[9]

---

[8] Chiara Lubich, *Essential Writings*, p. 190.
[9] Ibid.

Readings for *Lectio Divina*

Poem: 'The Dark Night'
(*Collected Works*, pages 358–9)

One dark night,
Fired with love's urgent longings
– Ah, the sheer grace! –
I went out unseen,
my house being now all stilled.

In darkness, and secure,
by secret ladder, disguised,
– Ah, the sheer grace! –
in darkness and concealment,
my house being now all stilled.

On that glad night,
in secret, for no one saw me,
nor did I look at anything,
with no other light or guide
than the one that burned in my heart.

This guided me
more surely than the light of noon
to where he was awaiting me
– him I knew so well –
there in a place where no one appeared.

O guiding night!
O night more lovely than the dawn!
O night that has united
the Lover with his beloved,
transforming the beloved in her Lover.

Upon my flowering breast
which I kept wholly for him alone,
there he lay sleeping,
and I caressing him
there in a breeze from the fanning cedars.

When the breeze blew from the turret,
as I parted his hair,
it wounded my neck
with its gentle hand,
suspending all my senses.

I abandoned and forgot myself,
laying my face on my Beloved;
all things ceased; I went out from myself,
leaving my cares
forgotten among the lilies.

The Dark Night, Book 1, Chapter 10, paragraphs 1–3 (*Collected Works,* page 381)

At the time of the aridities of this sensory night, God makes the exchange we mentioned by withdrawing the soul from the life of the senses and placing it in that of the spirit – that is, he brings it from meditation to contemplation – where the soul no longer has the power to work or meditate with its faculties on the things of God. Spiritual persons suffer considerable affliction in this night, owing not so much to the aridities they undergo as to their fear of having gone astray. Since they do not find any support or satisfaction in good things, they believe there will be no more spiritual blessings for them and that God has abandoned them.

They grow weary and strive, as was their custom, to concentrate their faculties with some satisfaction on a subject of meditation, and they think that if they do not do this and do not feel that they are at work, they are doing nothing. This effort of theirs is accompanied by an interior reluctance and repugnance on the part of the soul, for it would be pleased to dwell in that quietude and idleness without working with the faculties.

They consequently impair God's work and do not profit by their own. In searching for spirit, they lose the spirit that was the source of their tranquillity and peace. They are like someone who turns from what has already been done in order to do it again, or like one who leaves a city only to re-enter it, or they are like a hunter who abandons the prey in order to go hunting again. It is useless, then, for the soul to try to meditate because it will no longer profit by this exercise.

If there is no one to understand these persons, they either turn back and abandon the road or lose courage, or at least they hinder their own progress because of their excessive diligence in treading the path of discursive meditation. They fatigue and overwork themselves, thinking that they are failing because of their negligence or sins. Meditation is now useless for them because God is conducting them along another road, which is contemplation and is very different from the first, for the one road belongs to discursive meditation and the other is beyond the range of the imagination and discursive reflection.

Those who are in this situation should feel comforted; they ought to persevere patiently and not be afflicted. Let them trust in God who does not fail those who seek him with a simple and righteous heart; nor will he fail to impart what is needful for the way until getting them to the clear and pure light of love. God will give them this light by means of that other night, the night of spirit, if they merit that he place them in it.

The Dark Night, Book One, Chapter 10, paragraphs 4–6
(*Collected Works,* page 382)

The attitude necessary in the night of sense is to pay no attention to discursive meditation since this is not the time for it. They should allow the soul to remain in rest and quietude even though it may seem obvious to them that they are doing nothing and wasting time, and even though they think this disinclination to think about anything is due to their laxity. Through patience and perseverance in prayer, they will be doing a great deal without activity on their part.

All that is required of them here is freedom of soul, that they liberate themselves from the impediment and fatigue of ideas and thoughts, and care not about thinking and meditating. They must be content simply with a loving and peaceful attentiveness to God, and live without the concern, without the effort, and without the desire to taste or feel him. All these desires disquiet the soul and distract it from the peaceful, quiet, and sweet idleness of the contemplation that is being communicated to it.

And even though more scruples come to the fore concerning the loss of time and the advantages of doing something else, since it cannot do anything or think of anything in prayer, the soul should endure them peacefully, as though going to prayer means remaining in ease and freedom of spirit. If individuals were to desire to do something themselves with their interior faculties, they would hinder and lose the goods that God engraves on their souls through that peace and idleness.

If a model for the painting or retouching of a portrait should move because of a desire to do something, the artist would be unable to finish and the work would be spoiled. Similarly, any operation, affection, or thought a soul might cling to when it wants to abide in interior peace and idleness would cause distraction and disquietude, and make it feel sensory dryness and emptiness. The more a person seeks support in knowledge and affection the more the soul will feel the lack of these, for this support cannot be supplied through these sensory means.

Accordingly such persons should not mind if the operations of their faculties are being lost to them;

they should desire rather that this be done quickly so that there may be no obstacle to the operation of the infused contemplation God is bestowing, so that they may receive it with more peaceful plenitude and make room in the spirit for the enkindling and burning of the love that this dark and secret contemplation bears and communicates to the soul. For contemplation is nothing else than a secret and peaceful and loving inflow of God, which, if not hampered, fires the soul in the spirit of love, as is brought out in the following verse:

Fired with love's urgent longings.

CHAPTER FOUR

Brother Lawrence of the Resurrection

The Practice of the Presence of God

Nicholas Herman was born in Hériménil, Lorraine, France, probably in 1614. His parents were devout, and he was brought up in a religious atmosphere. At the age of eighteen he became a soldier in the forces of the Count of Lorraine and took part in the Thirty Years War. Having been wounded in the war, he returned home and worked for some time as a footman to a nobleman. This work did not suit him very well because, as he said himself, he was clumsy and broke things. His experience of the war had also made him disillusioned with life, so he decided to devote his life to Christ.

Nicholas spent some time as a hermit, but felt he needed a more structured life. He had an uncle who was a Carmelite, and he encouraged Nicholas to join the Carmelites. In 1640, Nicholas entered the Discalced Carmelite Monastery on the Rue de Vaugirard in Paris, where the Institut Catholique de Paris now stands. He was professed as a lay brother two years later and given the religious name Brother Lawrence of the Resurrection. Lawrence worked for many years in the kitchen of the monastery and later in the sandal repair shop. Occasionally he was sent on business errands for the monastery, such as going to Burgundy to buy wine.

During the first ten years of his life in the monastery, Brother Lawrence experienced great interior trials, similar to those described by St John of the Cross as the dark night. Then, one day, this gave way to a sense of peace and serenity that never left him. Gradually he gained a reputation for holiness. Many of the younger friars benefitted greatly from conversations with him. People also came to visit him in his workshop and ask his advice. One of these was the Abbé Joseph de Beaufort who compiled the book now known as *The Practice of the Presence of God* after Brother Lawrence's death. Brother Lawrence died at the monastery in Paris on 12 February 1691.

The Practice of the Presence of God
In 1666 and 1667, the Abbé Joseph de Beaufort had four conversations with Brother Lawrence that he wrote down. After Lawrence's death, he collected sixteen letters that the brother had written to various people and he also put together some notes or 'Spiritual Maxims' that Lawrence had made, summarising the advice he gave to those who asked him about his method of praying. The maxims and letters were published along with a biographical sketch of Brother Lawrence in 1692. The conversations were published two years later with a summary called the 'Ways of Brother Lawrence'. Most subsequent editions of *The Practice of the Presence of God* consist of the Conversations, Letters and Maxims. The Critical Edition[1] prepared by Conrad de Meester OCD and translated by Salvatore Sciurba OCD, presents the Maxims, Letters and Conversations in that order. I propose concentrating on the Letters and Conversations, as in them Brother Lawrence

---

[1] Brother Lawrence of the Resurrection OCD (Nicholas Herman), *Writings and Conversations on the Practice of the Presence of God,* Critical Edition by Conrad De Meester OCD, translated by Salvatore Sciurba OCD (Washington: ICS Publications, 1994).

comes to life more than in the Maxims, which contain the same teaching in more concise form. I will consider the Conversations first because they give us some insight into Brother Lawrence's life at a stage earlier than when he wrote the Letters.

The Conversations of Brother Lawrence with the Abbé Joseph de Beaufort

At the age of eighteen, around the time he joined the army, Brother Lawrence (or Nicholas as he was then called) had a profound experience which he referred to as his conversion. This is the Abbé de Beaufort's account.

> One day in winter while he was looking at a tree stripped of its leaves, and he realised that in a little while its leaves would reappear, followed by its flowers and fruit, he received a profound insight into God's providence that has never been erased from his soul. This insight completely freed him from the world and gave him such a love for God that he could not say it had increased during the more than forty years that had passed.[2]

Brother Lawrence's trust in Divine Providence was such that he did not allow the evils of the world to trouble him too much because he knew that God could remedy them whenever he saw fit.

The practice of the presence of God simply begins by turning to God frequently and talking to him. Brother Lawrence's advice was as follows:

> [He said] that we must establish ourselves in God's presence by continually conversing with him, and that it was shameful to give up conversation with him to turn to foolishness.[3]

---

[2] Brother Lawrence of the Resurrection, *op. cit.*, p. 89.
[3] Ibid.

His advice is simple, but it does involve mental discipline, especially at the beginning.

> [He said] that in the beginning we must work at forming the habit of continually conversing with God, attributing to him everything we do; but after a little effort we will feel ourselves awakened by love with no more difficulty.[4]

The main thing is to be direct and natural in our relationship with God.

> [He said] that we must act very straightforwardly with God, and speak to him freely, asking him for help in events as they happen, for God never fails to come to our aid, as he often experienced.[5]

Brother Lawrence says that the important thing is to keep trying. We should keep returning to the presence of God if we seem to have lost it. Lawrence could see that devotions and voluntary penances were all only means to an end, and only useful if they served that end which was the love of God and conformity to his will. He says, 'We settle for penances and private devotions, leaving aside love, our end'.[6]

One of the important points that Brother Lawrence makes is that we should not think of God only when we pray. We can be aware of the presence of God during work as well. We should do everything for the love of God. Again, the Abbé de Beaufort recounts what Lawrence said.

> He found no better way to approach God than by the ordinary works required in his case by obedience, purifying them as much as he could

---

[4] Brother Lawrence, *op. cit.*, p. 92.
[5] Ibid.
[6] Brother Lawrence, *op. cit.*, p. 96.

from all human respect, and doing them for the pure love of God. [He said] that it is a big mistake to think that the period of mental prayer should be different from any other. We must be just as closely united with God during our activities as we are during our times of prayer.[7]

Lawrence's prayer had become very simple over the years. He told his friend that, for him, 'mental prayer had become the experience of God's presence, his soul having withdrawn from everything except love'.[8] Love, in fact, is the key to everything. It is what gives value to all we do, no matter how small. Lawrence says: 'We must never tire of doing little things for the love of God who considers not the magnitude of the work, but the love.'[9]

In order to be authentic, the practice of the presence of God must be accompanied by a desire to do God's will and a commitment to give up anything that is contrary to God's will. It is also necessary to abandon oneself completely to God and trust in his Providence. So, despite its simplicity, the practice is demanding. Like St Teresa of Ávila before him, Brother Lawrence sees prayer in the context of living the Christian life in its fullness. Like St Thérèse after him, his way is one of confidence and love.

> We must cultivate faith, hope and love, for these alone can conform us completely to the will of God. All other things are insignificant, and we must not settle for them, but rather regard them as a bridge to be crossed quickly so we can lose ourselves in our sole end by confidence and love.[10]

---

[7] Brother Lawrence, *op. cit.*, p. 98.
[8] Ibid.
[9] Ibid.
[10] Ibid.

Letters

Sixteen letters written by Brother Lawrence between 1682 and 1691 have survived. When the Abbé de Beaufort published them, he replaced the names of the recipients with an *N* and indicated their state of life with headings, such as 'To a Nun', 'To the Same Nun', 'To a Priest', etc. These letters give us a real insight into Lawrence, his concern for others, the kind of practical advice that he gave and his prayer life.

The longest letter is written to an unknown priest who was probably a member of his Order, and upon whom he relied as a wise guide. It is possibly in this letter that Lawrence gives the fullest account of his inner life because he values the priest's judgement and is anxious to hear from him that he is following the right course. He tells him that during the first ten years of his religious life, despite his faith that never wavered, he suffered greatly from anxiety and feelings of unworthiness. Once he accepted that he might have to suffer this trial always, he was freed from it.

> Since that time, I do my work in simple faith before God, humbly and lovingly, and I carefully apply myself to avoid doing, saying, or thinking anything that might displease him. I hope that having done all I can, he will do with me as he pleases.[11]

Lawrence describes his prayer life as follows.

> I gave up all devotions and prayers that were not required and I devote myself exclusively to remaining always in his holy presence. I keep myself in his presence by simple attentiveness and a general awareness of God that I call 'actual

---

[11] Brother Lawrence, *op. cit.*, p. 53.

presence of God' or better, a quiet and secret conversation of the soul with God that is lasting.[12]

Lawrence says that he cannot doubt that his soul has been with God for more than thirty years. He considers himself to be the most miserable of human beings, deserving to be punished by God for his sins, but instead of chastising him, God lovingly embraces him and showers favours on him.

> My most typical approach is this simple attentiveness and general loving awareness of God, from which I derive greater sweetness and satisfaction than an infant receives from his mother's breast.[13]

Lawrence believed that through prayer he was gradually being transformed, that the image of God, which is in every human soul, was being brought to perfection.

> Sometimes I think of myself as a piece of stone before a sculptor who desires to carve a statue; presenting myself in this way before God I ask him to fashion his perfect image in my soul, making me entirely like himself.[14]

It is clear from his account that Lawrence experienced a high degree of contemplative prayer.

> At other times, as soon as I apply myself, I feel my whole mind and soul raised without trouble or effort, and it remains suspended and permanently rooted in God as in its centre and place of rest.[15]

---

[12] Brother Lawrence, *op. cit.*, p. 53.
[13] Ibid., p. 54.
[14] Ibid.
[15] Ibid.

He goes on to say that some people would call this state idleness, self-deception and self-love. He says he cannot agree with this and he asks the priest to tell him what he thinks: 'I would appreciate it if you would let me know your impression of this. It would mean a great deal to me for I have a special regard for you, Reverend Father.'[16] There are always those who are suspicious of mysticism, and it may well be that the occasion for Brother Lawrence's letter was some criticism of this kind that he had received.

Letter 12 is particularly interesting. It was sent to a nun who would appear to have been the prioress of one of Lawrence's correspondents. In the previous letter, Letter 11, he had asked the sister to whom he was writing to pass on his regards to Reverend Mother Prioress. In those days all correspondence passed through the hands of the prioress and she apparently found the advice Lawrence had given to the sister very interesting and wrote to him herself asking him to explain his method of prayer. His reply is a succinct account of his practice. He begins by addressing the issue directly.

> I will share with you the method I have used to arrive at this state of awareness of God's presence that our Lord in his mercy has granted me, since you insist that I do so.[17]

He admits that he is reluctant to do this. In an earlier letter to another sister, he had talked about the experience of a certain friar in his community, because he was reluctant to identify the friar as himself. This time he is more direct, perhaps because he recognises the prioress as a person of authority or because he feels himself near to death, as he confided

---

[16] Brother Lawrence, *op. cit.*, p. 55.
[17] Ibid., p. 75.

to the sister in Letter 11, and thinks it is important to share what he has learned from experience.

Lawrence says he found the various methods he found in books unhelpful, because they did not help him to do what he desired, which was to dispose himself completely to God.

> Thus, after offering myself entirely to God in atonement for my sins, I renounced for the sake of his love everything other than God, and I began to live as if only he and I existed in the world.[18]

Having put God at the centre of his life, Lawrence's method was to turn to God as often as possible.

> Sometimes I considered myself before him as a miserable criminal at his judge's feet, and at other times I regarded him in my heart as my Father, as my God. I adored him there as often as I could, keeping my mind in his holy presence, and recalling him as many times as I was distracted.[19]

He did not find this practice easy at the beginning, but persevered in it, during times set apart for prayer and when he was at work. He did not get upset when distracted, but simply returned to the practice. The practice brings great graces and becomes natural after a while.

> When we faithfully keep ourselves in his holy presence, seeing him always before us, not only avoiding offending or displeasing him – at least deliberately – but considering him in this

---

[18] Brother Lawrence, *op. cit.*, p. 75.
[19] Ibid.

fashion, we take the liberty to ask him for the graces we need. So, by repeating these acts they become familiar, and the practice of the presence of God becomes more natural.[20]

Brother Lawrence's last four letters were written to a nun, a Daughter of the Blessed Sacrament, between November 1690 and February 1691. The letters she sent to him have not survived, but it is apparent that she wrote to him telling him of the severe and painful illness from which she was suffering. In the first of the four letters, Lawrence tells the sister to offer her sufferings to God and to try to converse with him.

> God has various ways to draw us to himself. He sometimes hides from us, but faith alone – never lacking when needed – must be our support and the foundation of our trust, which must be placed entirely in God.[21]

It seems that in her next letter the sister must have told Lawrence about the various remedies she had tried to cure her illness, none of which had worked, because his advice is as follows.

> I think you should give up all human remedies and abandon yourself completely to divine providence; perhaps God is only waiting for this abandonment and for a perfect trust in him to cure you.[22]

He goes on to say that God sometimes permits physical suffering for the good of our souls and he encourages the sister to endure the suffering for the love of God.

---

[20] Brother Lawrence, *op. cit.*, p. 76.
[21] Ibid., p. 77.
[22] Ibid., p. 79.

> Love lightens suffering, and when we love God, we suffer for him joyfully and courageously; accept it I beg you. Find consolation in him who is the one and only remedy for all our troubles.[23]

This advice seems to have had the desired effect, because in the following letter Lawrence is thanking the Lord for relieving the sister's pain.

The fourth and final letter in this correspondence to the Daughter of the Blessed Sacrament is dated 6 February 1691, and so was written six days before Brother Lawrence died on 12 February. His closing words are as follows.

> Let us commit ourselves entirely to him [God] and banish everything else from our hearts and minds. He wants to be alone there, so we should ask him for this grace. If we do what we can, we will soon see the change we hope for in ourselves. I cannot thank him enough for the relief he has given you. I hope for the merciful grace of seeing him in a few days. Let us pray for each other.[24]

The practice of the presence of God begins by simply turning to God as often as possible and speaking to him very simply. Then one keeps returning to this awareness, reminding oneself of God's presence: God is always present to me; he is looking at me; he is listening to me. It is I who need to make myself present to God. Like St Teresa of Ávila, Brother Lawrence tells us to turn inward. This practice takes some effort at the beginning, but after a while there is an opening up and the sense of presence becomes habitual.

---

[23] Brother Lawrence, *op. cit.*, p. 79.
[24] Ibid., pp. 83–4.

What St Teresa calls 'recollection' and Brother Lawrence calls 'practice of the presence' are really the same thing. Brother Lawrence's special contribution is to emphasise the idea that one can be permanently recollected, whether at prayer or at work or in conversation with other people. In its emphasis on doing ordinary little things for love of God, his teaching anticipates that of St Thérèse of Lisieux.

Dialogue with Chiara Lubich

In her meditation 'Christ will be my cloister' Chiara Lubich shows that she is aware of the presence of God in a way that is very similar to that of Brother Lawrence.

> The Lord is within me, he would like to inspire my actions, to permeate my thought with his light, to arouse my will, to give me the law of my movements and of my stillness. But there is myself which, at times, does not allow him to live in me. If it stops interfering, God himself will take possession of my whole being and will know how to give the importance of an abbey to these walls and the sacredness of a church to this room, the harmony of liturgy to my meal and the perfume of a blessed habit to my clothes; the joyous note of a meeting with my brothers to the sound of the telephone or the doorbell, a meeting which interrupts yet continues my dialogue with God.[25]

---

[25] Chiara Lubich, *Meditations* (London: New City, 1975), pp. 88–9.

Readings for *Lectio Divina*

Fourth Conversation with the Abbé Beaufort, 25 November 1667, Extract: paragraphs 42–6, 49
(Critical Edition, pages 97–8)

Brother Lawrence spoke to me with great fervour and openness of his way of approaching God, as I have in part already noted. He told me that what matters is renouncing once and for all everything that we recognise does not lead to God, in order to become accustomed to a continual conversation with him, without mystery or finesse. We need only to recognise him present within us, to speak with him at every moment, and to ask for his help, so that we will know his will in perplexing events, and will be able to carry out those things we clearly see he asks of us, offering them to him before doing them, and thanking him afterward for completing them. During this continual conversation we are thus taken up in praising, adoring, and ceaselessly loving God for his infinite goodness and perfection.

We must ask him for his grace with full confidence, paying no attention to our thoughts, relying on the infinite merits of Our Lord. God, at every opportunity, always bestows his grace. Brother Lawrence saw this clearly and lacked this awareness only when he was distracted from God's company, or if he had forgotten to ask him for his help. In times of doubt God always gives light so long as our only concern is to please him and to act for the sake of his love.

He said that our sanctification depends not on our changing our works, but on doing for God what we would normally do for ourselves. It is a pity to see how many people are attached to certain works that they perform rather imperfectly and for human respect, always mistaking the means for the end.

He found no better way to approach God than by the ordinary works required in his case by obedience, purifying them as much as he could from all human respect, and doing them for the pure love of God.

[He said] that it is a big mistake to think that the period of mental prayer should be different from any other. We must be just as closely united with God during our activities as we are during our times of prayer.

We must never tire of doing little things for the love of God who considers not the magnitude of the work, but the love. In the beginning we must not be surprised if we often fail; in the end, once the habit is formed, we will be able to act without thinking about it and with great delight.

Letter 2: To a Spiritual Director, Extract
(Critical Edition, page 53. This is Letter 5 in other editions.)

When I accepted the fact that I might spend my life suffering from these troubles and anxieties – which in no way diminished the trust I had in God and served only to increase my faith – I found myself changed all at once. And my soul, until that time always in turmoil, experienced a deep inner peace as if it had found its centre and place of rest.

Since that time, I do my work in simple faith before God, humbly and lovingly, and I carefully apply myself to avoid doing, saying, or thinking anything that might displease him. I hope that having done all I can, he will do with me as he pleases.

I cannot express to you what is taking place in me at present. I feel neither concern nor doubt about my state since I have no will other than the will of God, which I try to carry out in all things and to which I am so surrendered that I would not so much as pick up a straw from the ground against his order, nor for any other reason than pure love.

I gave up all devotions and prayers that were not required and I devote myself exclusively to remaining always in his holy presence. I keep myself in his presence by simple attentiveness and a general awareness of God that I call 'actual presence of God' or better, a quiet and secret conversation of the soul with God that is lasting. This sometimes results in interior, and often exterior, contentment and joys so great that I have to perform childish acts, appearing more like folly than devotion, to control them and keep them from showing outwardly.

Therefore, Reverend Father, I cannot doubt at all that my soul has been with God for more than thirty years.

Letter 12: To a Nun
(Critical Edition, pages 75–6)

Reverend Mother,

I will share with you the method I have used to arrive at this state of awareness of God's presence that our Lord in his mercy has granted me, since you insist that I do so. I cannot hide the repugnance I feel in yielding to your request, even under the condition that you show my letter to no one. If I thought you would let someone see it, all the desire I have for your perfection would not make me comply. This is what I can tell you about it.

In several books I found different methods to approach God and various practices of the spiritual life that I feared would burden my mind rather than facilitate what I wanted and what I sought, namely, a means of being completely disposed to God. This led me to resolve to give all for all. Thus, after offering myself entirely to God in atonement for my sins, I renounced for the sake of his love everything other than God, and I began to live as if only he and I existed in the world. Sometimes I considered myself before him as a miserable criminal at his judge's feet, and at other times I regarded him in my heart as my

Father, as my God. I adored him there as often as I could, keeping my mind in his holy presence, and recalling him as many times as I was distracted. I had some trouble doing this exercise, but continued in spite of all the difficulties I encountered, without getting disturbed or anxious when I was involuntarily distracted. I was as faithful to this practice during my activities as I was during my periods of mental prayer, for at every moment, all the time, in the most intense periods of my work I banished and rid from my mind everything that was capable of taking the thought of God away from me.

This, Reverend Mother, is the devotion I have practiced since I entered religious life. Although I have practiced it feebly and imperfectly, I have nonetheless received many advantages from it. I certainly know this is due to the Lord's mercy and goodness – and this must be acknowledged – since we can do nothing without him, myself even less than others. But when we faithfully keep ourselves in his holy presence, seeing him always before us, not only avoiding offending or displeasing him – at least deliberately – but considering him in this fashion, we take the liberty to ask him for the graces we need. So, by repeating these acts they become familiar, and the practice of the presence of God becomes more natural. Join me in thanking him, please, for his great goodness to me, for I cannot esteem highly enough the great number of graces he bestows on me, a miserable sinner. May he be blessed by all. *Amen.* I am in our Lord,
Yours,

CHAPTER FIVE

Saint Thérèse of Lisieux

Her Family and Spiritual Brothers

Thérèse Martin was born in Alençon, Normandy, France, on 2 January 1873. She was baptised two days later at the church of Notre-Dame and given the name Marie-Françoise-Thérèse. She was the last of nine children born to Louis Martin and his wife Zélie Guérin, both of whom are now recognised as saints by the Catholic Church. Four of their children, two boys and two girls, died in infancy or early childhood.

Thérèse had four surviving sisters. Marie was the eldest and regarded as quite independent-minded. She was thirteen years older than Thérèse. She became the mistress of the household when Zélie died. Marie was Thérèse's godmother and prepared her for her First Communion. Pauline, who was twelve years older than Thérèse, was next. When Zélie died, Thérèse chose Pauline to be her mother. She was also to become her prioress for three years in the convent. Leonie was the girl in the middle, ten years older than Thérèse. She had some learning difficulties when she was young, but she helped care for their father Louis when he became old and infirm. She gave Thérèse a crucifix which she always treasured and kept with her. Céline was four years older than Thérèse and was her inseparable companion and friend. All five Martin girls became nuns. Four of them entered the Carmel in Lisieux. Leonie joined the Visitation Order in Caen.

I mention these details because they help us to understand where Thérèse was coming from. She was very close to her parents and sisters. Hers was a devout Catholic family. Both Louis and Zélie had tried to enter religious life but were not accepted. They had hoped that their little boys would become priests and missionaries. They attended daily Mass, had family prayers and observed the feasts and fasts of the Church. It is refreshing, all the same, to read that Zélie remarks in a letter to her sister that she wished Lent was over as she did not like it. As well as being the homemaker for the family, Zélie had her own lace-making business. Louis was a watchmaker. He was an active member of the St Vincent de Paul Society. In his spare time, he liked to fish. Zélie's health was already in decline when Thérèse was born. She had breast cancer. She involved Marie in the running of the household because she knew that Marie might have to take on the role of homemaker before long. Zélie did not want to die; she wanted to be there for her children. Two months before her death, Zélie and the three older girls went on a pilgrimage to Lourdes to pray for a cure.

Thérèse was four and a half years old when her mother died in 1877. Zélie's death had a devastating effect on the whole family and especially on Thérèse. Later that year the family moved to Lisieux, where Zélie's brother Isidore had a pharmacy. They took up residence in 'Les Buissonnets', which was a spacious house with a fine garden.

Up to the time of her mother's death Thérèse had been a happy child, doted on by her parents and sisters. Now she became withdrawn and oversensitive and suffered from a series of psychosomatic illnesses. The worst of these was in April and May of 1883 when Thérèse was ten. The family feared that she was dying and prayed to Our Lady for a cure. Looking at a statue of the Blessed Virgin in the room, Thérèse had an experience of Our Lady smiling at her and she was cured. Thérèse realised that the Blessed Virgin was a mother who would never leave her. Pauline, who had replaced Zélie as Thérèse's mother, had entered the Lisieux Carmel the previous October. The statue is now located above Thérèse's tomb and known as Our Lady of the Smile. The following year, Thérèse made her First Holy Communion in May and received Confirmation in June.

The cure of Thérèse's mysterious illness was not the end of her troubles. For a year and a half, from 1885 to 1886, she suffered from scruples, which she describes as a martyrdom. The spiritual atmosphere in France in the nineteenth century is often described as Jansenistic. This is not really accurate, as Jansenism was well gone, having been condemned by Pope Innocent X in 1653 and, again, by Pope Clement XI in 1713. It would be more accurate to call the spirituality of the time Neo-Pelagian, the idea that we can save ourselves by our own efforts. Jansenism did leave a certain legacy, however, in a kind of merciless moral perfectionism and in an image of God as remote, austere and demanding. The result was a recipe for neurosis. Thérèse would later provide the antidote to this in her understanding of God as merciful Love.

Thérèse's self-absorption and nervous troubles suddenly came to an end on Christmas Eve 1886, shortly before her fourteenth birthday. Having returned from Midnight Mass and eager to find her presents, Thérèse overheard her father, tired and a little irritated, saying, 'Well, fortunately, this will be the last year!' Normally, Thérèse would have burst into tears, but she received the grace to control her feelings and from then on was no longer the oversensitive child she had been. She says, 'Thérèse had discovered once again the strength of soul which she had lost at the age of four and a half, and she was to preserve it forever.' She goes on to say, 'I felt *charity* enter into my soul, and the need to forget myself and to please others; since then I have been happy!'[1]

Vocation to Carmel

Thérèse felt attracted to the life of Carmel from the time Pauline had entered there, not in order to be with Pauline, although she missed her terribly, but in order to give her life to Jesus. Pauline had tried to explain to her little sister why she was entering Carmel and she described it so beautifully that Thérèse wanted to do the same. Now it became clear to her that this was her vocation. By now Thérèse had two sisters in Carmel, as Marie had entered earlier in the year.

Thérèse's vocation took on an apostolic aspect from the start. She wanted to bring others to God. The first person that caught her attention, and became the object of her prayer, was Henri Pranzini, a convicted murderer who had been sentenced to death. According to reports he was unrepentant. Thérèse prayed for his conversion.

> Feeling that of myself I could do nothing, I offered to God all the infinite merits of Our Lord, the treasures of the Church, and finally I begged Céline to have a Mass offered for my intentions.[2]

She asked for some sign that Pranzini had turned to God before the end. He was executed by guillotine on 31 August 1887. Thérèse sneaked a look at next day's edition of *La Croix* newspaper to see what had happened.

---

[1] Saint Thérèse of Lisieux, *Story of a Soul,* translated by John Clark OCD (Washington: ICS Publications, 1996), pp. 98–9.
[2] Saint Thérèse of Lisieux, *Story of a Soul,* p. 99.

Pranzini had not gone to confession. He had mounted the scaffold and was prepared to place his head in the formidable opening, when suddenly, seized by an inspiration, he turned, took hold of the *crucifix* the priest was holding out to him and *kissed* the *sacred wounds three times!* Then his soul went to receive the *merciful* sentence of Him who declares that in heaven there will be more joy over one sinner who does penance than over ninety-nine just who have no need of repentance.[3]

Thérèse did not want to waste time; she wanted to enter Carmel as soon as possible. Her father was the easiest person to convince. The prioress and the bishop were not so easy to convince, but Thérèse succeeded after much persuasion. She even asked Pope Leo XIII to allow her to enter early when she accompanied her father and Céline on a pilgrimage to Rome with a group from Lisieux.

Saint Thérèse and Missionary Priests

Thérèse's interest in the missions began with her parents. As mentioned, four of Louis and Zélie's children died before Thérèse was born. Hélène was born in 1864. That she lived to the age of five meant that her death caused great sadness to her parents. After Hélène, two boys were born: Joseph-Louis was born in 1866 and lived for five months. Joseph-Jean-Baptiste was born the following year and lived for nine months. Mélanie-Thérèse came in-between the births of Céline and Thérèse and lived for two months. When the first of the boys was born, Louis and Zélie hoped that he would become a priest and missionary. They had the same hopes for the second. It is probably to these brothers that she never met,

_____

[3] Saint Thérèse of Lisieux, *Story of a Soul*, p. 100.

but whose memory was kept alive in the family, that Thérèse refers when she writes as follows.

> I want to be a daughter of the Church as our holy Mother St Teresa was and to pray for the Holy Father's intentions which I know embrace the whole universe. This is the general purpose of my life, but this would not have prevented me from praying and uniting myself in a special way to the works of my dear little angels if they had become priests.[4]

In the examination preceding her profession, when asked why she had come to Carmel, Thérèse replied, 'I came to save souls and especially, to pray for priests'.[5] In her letter to her sister Marie ('Manuscript B' in the autobiography), she writes:

> I have the *vocation of the Apostle.* ... I would want to preach the Gospel on all five continents simultaneously and even to the remotest isles. I would be a missionary, not for a few years only, but from the beginning of creation until the consummation of the ages.[6]

In 1895, when Mother Agnes (Thérèse's sister Pauline) was prioress, she received a letter from a seminarian, Maurice Bellière, requesting that one of the nuns pray for him particularly. He was a student in the diocesan seminary, but he was hoping to be accepted for the missions. Mother Agnes asked Thérèse to take on the task of praying for Maurice. At first, he corresponded with Mother Agnes, but then when Mother Marie de Gonzague resumed the role of prioress, she asked

---

[4] Saint Thérèse of Lisieux, *Story of a Soul,* pp. 253–4.
[5] Ibid., p. 149.
[6] Ibid., pp. 192–3.

Thérèse to write to him directly herself. A very special friendship developed between them. Maurice was one year her junior and she called him her 'little brother'. In her third letter to him she says:

> Truly, you will know only in heaven how dear you are to me; I feel our souls are made to understand one another.[7]

They became true 'soul friends', as the Irish term *anamchara* expresses it. Maurice was a young man who was very unsure of himself and Thérèse gave him encouragement and affirmation. In one of her letters to Maurice, Thérèse compares their relationship to that of St Margaret Mary Alocoque and St Claude La Colombière. Saint Margaret Mary had had a vision of their two hearts united in the Sacred Heart of Jesus.

> Perhaps, Brother, the comparison does not appear fair to you? It is true that you are not yet a Père de la Colombière, but I do not doubt that one day, you will be a real apostle of Christ like him. As for myself, the thought does not come into my mind to compare myself with Blessed Margaret Mary. I simply state that Jesus has chosen me to be the sister of one of His apostles.[8]

Thérèse recommended the same 'little way' to her 'little brother' that she had learned herself.

> Ah! How little known are the goodness, the merciful love of Jesus, Brother! ... It is true, to

---

[7] Saint Thérèse of Lisieux, *Letters: General Correspondence*, translated by John Clark OCD (Washington: ICS Publications, 1988), Vol. 2, p. 1059.
[8] Ibid., p. 1084.

enjoy these treasures one must humble oneself, recognise one's nothingness, and that is what many souls do not want to do; but, little Brother, this is not the way you act, so the way of simple and loving confidence is really made for you.[9]

Thérèse was allowed keep a photograph of Maurice. This was an unusual privilege in those days when Carmelite nuns were not even allowed pictures of their relatives. On her death, Thérèse left him a special relic she received at her profession and the crucifix that her sister Leonie had given her at the age of thirteen and which she always kept with her. Thérèse and Maurice never met in person in this life. He was ordained for the White Fathers in 1901 and worked for some years in Nyassa, Africa. He returned to France in 1906 due to ill health and died at Caen the following year, aged thirty-three.

In May 1896, Thérèse was assigned a second spiritual brother by Mother Marie de Gonzague. Adolphe Roulland was ordained to the priesthood in June of the same year for the Foreign Mission Society of Paris and sailed for the mission in China in August. On 3 July 1896 he celebrated Mass at the Carmel in Lisieux and met Sister Thérèse. Thérèse had his photograph and a map of the mission in China where he was working. In one of her early letters she copied out some of her favourite passages from the Prophet Isaiah and she ended with the following assurance.

A Dieu, Brother ... distance will never be able to separate our souls, death itself will make our union more intimate. If I go to heaven soon, I will ask Jesus' permission to go to visit you

---

[9] Saint Thérèse of Lisieux, *Letters: General Correspondence*, Vol. 2, p. 1165.

at Su-Tchuen, and we shall continue our apostolate together.[10]

In one of his letters, Père Roulland expresses the fear that he would go to purgatory if he were to be killed on the mission. Thérèse's reply shows her profound understanding of the relationship between God's justice and his mercy. As she sees it, God is merciful because he is just. His justice makes him take our weakness into account.

> I expect as much from God's justice as from His mercy. It is because He is just that 'He is compassionate and filled with gentleness, slow to punish, and abundant in mercy, for He knows our frailty, He remembers that we are dust'.[11]

Thérèse assures him that she believes he would go straight to heaven because, as a missionary, he has dedicated his life to God.

> It seems to me that all missionaries are martyrs by desire and will and that, as a consequence, not one should have to go to purgatory.[12]

In her last letter to her missionary brother, she assures him that she will continue to help him when she is in heaven.

> I really count on not remaining inactive in heaven. My desire is to work still for the Church and for souls. I am asking God for this and I am certain that He will answer me.

---

[10] Saint Thérèse of Lisieux, *Letters: General Correspondence*, Vol. 2, p. 978.
[11] Ibid., p. 1093.
[12] Ibid.

Brother, you will not have time to send me your messages for heaven, but I am guessing at them, and then you will only have to tell me them in a whisper, and I shall hear you, and I shall carry your messages faithfully to the Lord, to our Immaculate Mother, to the Angels and to the Saints whom you love.[13]

Père Roulland continued to work in China until 1909 when he was recalled to France. He died in 1934, aged sixty-four.

Saint Thérèse was canonised in 1925 by Pope Pius XI. In 1927, thirty years after her death, the same pope proclaimed her Patroness of the Missions.

Dialogue with Chiara Lubich

The charism of the Focolare Movement is unity. Thérèse would have appreciated this very well. She lived in unity with her spiritual brothers. This is clear from the passage she quoted for Maurice from the *Life* of St Margaret Mary and applied to their relationship.

One day, when I was approaching Our Lord to receive Him in Holy Communion, He showed His Sacred Heart as a burning furnace and two other hearts (her own and that of P. de la Colombière) that were about to be united and engulfed in It, saying: 'It is thus that My pure love unites three hearts forever'.[14]

Thérèse kept nothing for herself. All her prayers and sacrifices were for the Church and its mission in the world. She was also aware of Jesus in the midst, especially during prayer in common. Her spirituality

---

[13] Saint Thérèse of Lisieux, *Letters: General Correspondence*, Vol. 2, p. 1142.
[14] Ibid., p. 1084.

has been interpreted in an individualistic way, but it is open to the idea of a communal spirituality.

Readings for *Lectio Divina*

Story of a Soul, Manuscript A, Chapter 5, pages 98–9

It was 25 December 1886 that I received the grace of leaving my childhood, in a word, the grace of my complete conversion. We had come back from Midnight Mass where I had the happiness of receiving the *strong* and *powerful* God. Upon arriving at Les Buissonnets, I used to love to take my shoes from the chimney corner and examine the presents in them; this old custom had given us so much joy in our youth that Céline wanted to continue treating me as a baby since I was the youngest in the family. Papa had always loved to see my happiness and listen to my cries of delight as I drew each surprise from the *magic shoes,* and my dear King's gaiety increased my own happiness very much. However, Jesus desired to show me that I was to give up the defects of my childhood and so He withdrew its innocent pleasures. He permitted Papa, tired out after the Midnight Mass, to experience annoyance when seeing my shoes at the fireplace, and that he speak those words which pierced my heart: 'Well, fortunately, this will be the last year!' I was going upstairs, at the time, to remove my hat, and Céline, knowing how sensitive I was and seeing the tears already glistening in my eyes, wanted to cry too, for she loved me very much and understood my grief. She said, 'Oh, Thérèse, don't go downstairs; it would cause you too much grief to look at your slippers right now!' But Thérèse was no longer the same; Jesus had changed her heart! Forcing back my tears I descended the stairs rapidly; controlling the poundings of my heart, I took my slippers and placed them in front of Papa, and withdrew all the objects joyfully. I had the happy appearance of a Queen. Having regained his own cheerfulness, Papa was laughing; Céline believed it was all a *dream*! Fortunately, it was a sweet reality; Thérèse had discovered once again the strength of soul which she had lost at the age of four and a half, and she was to preserve it forever!

On that *night of light* began the third period of my life, the most beautiful and the most filled with graces from heaven. The work I had been unable to do in ten years was done by Jesus in one instant, contenting himself with my *good will* which was never lacking. I could say to Him like his apostles: 'Master, I fished all night and caught nothing.' More merciful to me than He was with His disciples, Jesus *took the net Himself*, cast it, and drew it in filled with fish. He made me a fisher of *souls*. I experienced a great desire to work for the conversion of sinners, a desire I hadn't felt so intensely before.

I felt *charity* enter into my soul, and the need to forget myself and to please others; since then I have been happy!

Letter 261: From Thérèse to l'abbé Bellière, Extract
(*General Correspondence*, Volume 2, pages 1164–5)

You must know me only imperfectly to fear that a detailed account of your faults may diminish the tenderness I have for your soul! Oh, Brother, believe it, I shall have no need 'to place my hand on the lips of Jesus.' He has forgotten your infidelities now for a long time; only your desires for perfection are present to give joy to His Heart. I beg you do not *drag* yourself any longer to *His feet*; follow that 'first impulse that draws you into His arms.' That is where your place is, and I have learned, more so than in your other letters, that you are *forbidden* to go to heaven by any other way except that of your poor little sister.

I am in total agreement with your opinion: 'The divine Heart is more saddened by a thousand little indelicacies of His friends than by even the grave sins that persons of the world commit'; but, dear little Brother, it seems to me that it is *only* when His own, unaware of their continual indelicacies, make a habit of them and do not ask His pardon, that Jesus can say these touching words which are placed for us in His mouth by the Church during Holy Week: 'These wounds you see in my hands are the ones I received in the house of those who *loved me!*' Regarding those who *love* Him and who come after each indelicacy to ask His pardon by throwing themselves into His arms, Jesus is thrilled with joy. He says to His angels what the father of the prodigal son says to his servants: 'Clothe him in his best robe, and place a ring on his finger, and let us rejoice.' Ah! How little known are the *goodness*, the *merciful love* of Jesus, Brother! ... It is true, to enjoy these treasures one must humble oneself, recognise one's nothingness, and that is what many souls do not want to do; but, little Brother, this is not the way you act, so the way of simple and loving confidence is really made for you.

Letter 226: From Thérèse to Père Roulland, Extract
(*General Correspondence*, Volume 2, page 1093)

I do not understand, Brother, how you seem to doubt your immediate entrance into heaven if the infidels were to take your life. I know one must be very pure to appear before the God of all Holiness, but I know, too, that the Lord is infinitely just; and it is this justice which frightens so many souls that is the object of my joy and confidence. I expect as much from God's justice as from His mercy. It is because He is just that 'He is compassionate and filled with gentleness, slow to punish, and abundant in mercy, for He knows our frailty, He remembers that we are dust. As a father has tenderness for his children, so the Lord has compassion on us!' Oh, Brother, when hearing these beautiful and consoling words of the Prophet-King, how can we doubt that God will open the doors of His kingdom to His children who loved Him even to sacrificing all for Him, who have not only left their family and their country to make Him known and loved, but even desire to give their life for Him whom they love ... Jesus was very right in saying that there is no greater love than that! How would He allow Himself to be overcome in generosity? How would He purify in the flames of purgatory souls consumed in the fires of divine love? It is true that no human life is exempt from faults; only the Immaculate Virgin presents herself absolutely pure before the divine Majesty. Since she loves us and since she knows our weakness, what have we to fear? Here are a lot of sentences to express my thought, or rather not to succeed in expressing it, I wanted simply to say that it seems to me that all missionaries are *martyrs* by desire and will and that, as a consequence, not one should have to go to purgatory. If there remains in their soul at the moment of appearing before God some trace of human weakness, the Blessed Virgin obtains for them the grace of making an act of perfect love, and then she gives them the palm and the crown that they so greatly merited.

CHAPTER SIX

Saint Thérèse of Lisieux

Story of a Soul

Thérèse entered the Lisieux Carmel on 9 April 1888 and received the habit (the distinctive religious garb of the Order) on 10 January 1889. She took the name Sister Thérèse of the Child Jesus and the Holy Face. Her father Louis was present on these occasions, but shortly after Thérèse received the habit, he was hospitalised at an institution in Caen for those with mental illness. Léonie and Céline took lodgings at an orphanage in the town in order to be near him. The illness of their father was a cause of great suffering for all his daughters. He died in 1894, and later that year, Céline entered the Lisieux Carmel and was given the name Sister Geneviève of St Teresa. At that stage Thérèse was looking after the novices. Léonie became a Visitation Sister at Caen in 1899 after some previous unsuccessful attempts at religious life. She took the name Sister Françoise-Thérèse, combining the names of the founder of the Visitation Order (St Francis de Sales) with that of her sister, then in heaven.

The Lisieux Carmel was founded in 1838 from Poitiers. The foundress was Mother Geneviève of St Teresa. She was still alive when Thérèse entered. She died in 1891. Thérèse regarded her as a saint. Mother Marie de Gonzague was prioress from 1869 until 1902, apart from three years, 1893 to 1896, when

Mother Agnes of Jesus (Thérèse's sister Pauline) was prioress. Mother Marie de Gonzague was a very perceptive woman. She obviously saw something special in Thérèse, allowing her to enter the convent at the age of fifteen. She was strict, which was the ethos of the time. She was particularly strict with Thérèse at the beginning so that she would not be pampered by the community. As time went on, she recognised Thérèse's special gifts and gave her more responsibility. Mother Marie de Gonzague was broad-minded enough to allow Thérèse to correspond with her two spiritual brothers and have their photographs, something that would have been quite exceptional at the time. Mother Marie de Gonzague died in 1904. Mother Agnes was to succeed her in 1902 and continue as prioress (apart from an interval of eighteen months) until she died in 1951.

As well as the four Martin sisters, their first cousin, Marie Guérin, was also a member of the community. She was the daughter of Zélie's brother Isidore and his wife Céline. The two families were very close and spent much time together, especially after the Martins moved to Lisieux. Marie was three years older than Thérèse and became one of her novices. In religion, her name was Sister Marie of the Eucharist.

Saint Thérèse spent nine years in the Lisieux Carmel. She made a good contribution to the life of the community. She was loved and respected by the other nuns, but most of them were unaware of the depth of her spirituality. Her relationship with God was hidden. To both her prioresses, however, she was completely open as this was part of what was required of a Carmelite religious. Mother Marie de Gonzague's assessment of Thérèse at her profession at seventeen and a half was that she had the judgement of a woman of thirty and very good self-mastery. When Thérèse was twenty, she was able to describe Thérèse as follows:

A mystic, a *comedienne*, she is everything! She can make you shed tears of devotion, and she can as easily make you split your sides with laughter during recreation.[1]

Thérèse was quite creative. She wrote poetry and composed prayers. She also wrote a number of dramatic sketches and 'theatrical recreations'. In January 1894 she produced a play that she had written for the community on the life of Joan of Arc. She played Joan herself. She corresponded with a number of people. Two hundred and sixty-six of her letters have survived and have been published. She was involved in all the ordinary tasks of life in the convent, such as sweeping the floors, acting as sacristan and caring for the sick. Her kindness to the sick was particularly remembered. It was in the ordinary tasks that she found holiness. In February 1893 she was put in charge of the novices, although, because of her young age, she was not given the title of novice mistress. She taught them her 'little way' of abandonment to God and confidence in his merciful love. She believed that Our Lord had taught her this way himself, not through any revelations, but by experience.

At Easter in 1896, it became clear that Thérèse was seriously ill. On Holy Thursday night she was coughing up blood, which indicated that she was suffering from tuberculosis of the lungs. She was to continue her normal duties for another year, despite her illness. During this time, she also experienced the Night of Faith, a trial that enabled her to identify with unbelievers. At the end of Lent in 1897, Thérèse was dying and was moved to the infirmary where she

---

[1] Mother Marie de Gonzague, in a letter to the Visitation convent at Le Mans, quoted in *St. Thérèse of Lisieux: Her Last Conversations*, translated by John Clark OCD (Washington: ICS Publications, 1977), p. 16.

spent the last months of her life. She was cared for during this time by her sisters who wrote down many of the conversations they had with her. These were later published as *Her Last Conversations*. Sister Thérèse of the Child Jesus and the Holy Face died on 30 September 1897.

Story of a Soul

In a sense, the Martin sisters were a community within the Carmel community, and it is within this context that Thérèse's autobiography, *Story of a Soul*, came to be written. One evening at recreation in 1895, Thérèse was reminiscing with her two older sisters about her childhood. Marie (Sister Marie of the Sacred Heart) suggested that she should write an account of her childhood. Pauline (Mother Agnes), being then the prioress, and probably half in jest, told Thérèse that she was ordering her to write her memoirs. Thérèse took obedience very seriously and set to work. This explains why she applied herself to the task with such diligence and honesty. The style of writing was determined by her relationship with Pauline and contains many expressions of affection. It is addressed to her sister, whom she saw as her mother as well as her religious superior. The first part of Thérèse's autobiography, 'Manuscript A', was originally intended only for private circulation within the family. It took the best part of a year to write, as she only wrote during the time allotted to writing letters.

The second part of *Story of a Soul*, 'Manuscript B', was also written at Marie's request. During Thérèse's last retreat she asked her to write an account of her 'little doctrine'. Thérèse's reply contains not only her little doctrine, but how she came to understand her vocation to be 'love at the heart of the Church'. It is the shortest of the three manuscripts, but it contains some of the most significant passages in the whole autobiography.

Mother Agnes (Pauline) did not get around to reading Thérèse's account of her childhood and early years in Carmel until the summer of 1896, at which stage she was no longer prioress. She realised that what her sister had written was of value and might be of interest to a wider audience. She approached Mother Marie de Gonzague and suggested to her that she order Thérèse to complete the account of her life. At this stage Thérèse was already quite ill, but she complied. The result was 'Manuscript C', which is addressed to Mother Marie de Gonzague.

After Thérèse's death, Mother Agnes put the three manuscripts together, putting in chapter headings and editing as she saw fit. Thérèse had confided this task to her during her last illness. It was published in 1898 as *Histoire d'une Ame (Story of a Soul)* and was an immediate bestseller. After Mother Agnes's death in 1951, a new addition was brought out using the original manuscripts without Mother Agnes's editorial changes. Subsequently, more recent editions have incorporated her helpful chapter headings.

'Manuscript B'
Let us take a closer look at 'Manuscript B'. As mentioned, it was written at the request of her sister Marie (Sister Marie of the Sacred Heart) who was also Thérèse's godmother. It was written in September 1896 during a private retreat that Thérèse had undertaken. This was about a year before her death, which she knew would not be very long in coming. The manuscript begins as a letter to her sister and godmother, but then Thérèse addresses Jesus directly, as she finds this easier.

Sister Marie had asked her to explain her little doctrine and Thérèse begins by recalling a number of texts from the Old Testament where God invites the little ones to come to him. These include: 'Whoever is little, let him come to me' (Prov 9:4), 'He shall gather together the lambs with his arm and shall take them up in his bosom' (Is 40:11) and 'As one whom his mother caresses, so I will comfort you' (Is 66:12-13). The way of littleness means accepting that we are weak and imperfect and incapable of doing great things for God.

> Jesus does not demand great actions from us but simply *surrender* and *gratitude* ... He has no need of our works but only of our *love*.[2]

After this brief introduction, the rest of the letter is really an extended prayer. Thérèse recounts a dream she had in which she spoke to Venerable Anne of Jesus, one of the companions of St Teresa of Ávila, who brought the Carmelite nuns to France. She asked Venerable Anne whether she would die soon, to which she received the reply that she would, very soon. Then she asked whether God was content with her, or did he require more from her. Venerable Anne replied that God was very content.

Thérèse was writing on the sixth anniversary of her religious profession, so it was appropriate that she reflect on the meaning of this. She goes on to describe how she understands her vocation.

> To be Your Spouse, to be a Carmelite, and by my union with You to be the Mother of souls, should not this suffice me? ... And yet I feel within me other vocations. I feel the *vocation* of the WARRIOR, THE PRIEST, THE APOSTLE, THE DOCTOR, THE MARTYR.[3]

Thérèse says that she wanted to be all of these. She says her desires caused her a veritable martyrdom.

---

[2] Saint Thérèse of Lisieux, *Story of a Soul*, pp. 188–9.
[3] Ibid., p. 192.

Then she says that in her meditation she turned to the Epistles of St Paul and found his First Letter to the Corinthians. In Chapter 12 she read how the Church is made up of different members, that all cannot be apostles, prophets and teachers. This did not really answer her question, because she could see herself in all of these. In the next part of the letter, Chapter 13, St Paul goes on to show a more excellent way, the way of love. Thérèse recognised that this was the answer to her quest.

> I understood that if the Church had a body composed of different members, the most necessary and the most noble of all could not be lacking to it, and so I understood that the Church *had a Heart and that this Heart* was BURNING WITH LOVE.[4]

Thérèse could see that it was love that motivated the apostles, martyrs and all the vocations in the Church. Love includes all vocations.

> Then, in the excess of my delirious joy, I cried out: O Jesus, my Love ... my vocation, at last I have found it ... MY VOCATION IS LOVE! Yes, I have found my place in the Church and it is You, O my God, who have given me this place; in the heart of the Church, my Mother, I shall be *Love*.[5]

She goes on to say that it is not so much a delirious joy to have found her place in the Church, it is more the serene peace of the navigator arriving into port. This motivated Thérèse to offer herself as a victim to the merciful love of God.

---

[4] Saint Thérèse of Lisieux, *Story of a Soul*, p. 194.
[5] Ibid.

O Jesus, I know it, love is repaid by love alone, and so I searched, and I found the way to solace my heart by giving you Love for Love.[6]

An interesting point is Thérèse's understanding of the Church. She does not see it primarily as an institution, but as a living organism. This was nearly half a century before Pope Pius XII proposed this theology of the Church, based on the teaching of St Paul, in the encyclical *Mystici Corporis* (1943). Saint Thérèse was ahead of her time.

Saint Thérèse's main insight was that it is love that gives value to our works. Therefore, the smallest act can be of value if it is done out of love. Little souls are only capable of small acts, but they take on a great value when done for love. So, it is important not to miss the little opportunities that come each day to show love.

I have no other means of showing my love for you than that of strewing flowers, that is, not allowing one little sacrifice to escape, not one look, one word, profiting by all the smallest things and doing them through love.[7]

Thérèse quotes St John of the Cross, with whose works she was familiar.

The smallest act of PURE LOVE is of more value than all other works together.[8]

She goes on to use the comparison of the little bird and the eagle. She is the little bird. She cannot soar

---

[6] Saint Thérèse of Lisieux, *Story of a Soul,* p. 195.
[7] Ibid., p. 196.
[8] Saint Thérèse of Lisieux, *Story of a Soul,* p. 197, St John of the Cross, *Spiritual Canticle, Collected Works,* p. 587.

like the great saints who are the eagles. She can only chirp and flap her wings without flying, but she still wants to gaze at the sun. Sometimes, the little bird falls asleep or gets distracted (as Thérèse did during prayers), but it always comes back and asks forgiveness and begins again. This brings Thérèse to the other important point in her 'little way', that of abandonment and confidence.

> I feel that if You found a soul weaker and littler than mine, which is impossible, You would be pleased to grant it still greater favours, provided it abandoned itself with total confidence to Your Infinite Mercy.[9]

Saint Thérèse's 'little way' is a way of holiness for everyone. Sanctity is within reach of the ordinary person. In a note to Sr Marie, written a few days after giving her 'Manuscript B', Thérèse further emphasises littleness and confidence.

> Oh dear Sister, I beg you, understand your little girl, understand that to love Jesus, to be a *victim of love*, the weaker one is, without desires or virtues, the more suited one is for the workings of this consuming and transforming Love ... Let us love our littleness, let us love to feel nothing, then we shall be poor in spirit, and Jesus will come to look for us, and *however far* we may be, He will transform us in flames of love ... It is confidence and nothing but confidence that must lead us to Love.[10]

---

[9] Saint Thérèse of Lisieux, *Story of a Soul*, p. 200.
[10] Saint Thérèse of Lisieux, *Letters: General Correspondence*, Vol. 2, pp. 999–1000.

Saint Thérèse did not make a distinction between love of God and love of neighbour. The little act of love could be putting up with an irritating sister, smiling at someone who seemed depressed or just doing the ordinary chores.

Thérèse found that the long prayers in books gave her a headache. Her approach to prayer was very simple.

> I say very simply to God what I wish to say, without composing beautiful sentences, and He always understands me. For me *prayer* is an aspiration of the heart, it is a simple glance directed to heaven, it is a cry of gratitude and love in the midst of trial as well as joy; finally, it is something great, supernatural, which expands my soul and unites me to Jesus.[11]

Thérèse liked the Divine Office and regarded it as a privilege to recite it in choir. In common prayer she was aware of the support of her sisters.

> I love very much these prayers in common, for Jesus has promised *to be in the midst of those who gather together in His name.* I feel that the fervour of my Sisters makes up for my lack of fervour.[12]

Saint Teresa of Ávila wrote *The Way of Perfection.* Saint Thérèse's way could be called 'the Way of Imperfection' in the sense that she teaches us not to be discouraged by imperfection, but to use our imperfections to constantly look for God's mercy and to do the little we can, to do ordinary things, with love.

---

[11] Saint Thérèse of Lisieux, *Story of a Soul*, p. 242.
[12] Ibid.

Dialogue with Chiara Lubich

Chiara Lubich would have been familiar with St Thérèse's doctrine of the Little Way. In one of her 'Word of Life' reflections, her advice is very similar to that of St Thérèse.

> Jesus allows us to experience our limitations, not to discourage us, but to help us experience the extraordinary power of his grace, which reveals itself in those very moments when we cannot make it on our own strength, so that we can better understand his love. There is one condition, we need to have boundless trust in him, to feel that we are in the arms of a Father who loves us as we are and for whom everything is possible. We cannot be discouraged even by the knowledge of our mistakes because, being love, God picks us up every time that we fall down, as parents do with their children.[13]

Readings for *Lectio Divina*

Story of a Soul, Manuscript B, Chapter 9, pages 188–9

I understand so well that it is only love that makes us acceptable to God, that this love is the only good I ambition. Jesus deigned to show me the road that leads to this Divine Furnace, and this road is the *surrender* of the little child who sleeps without fear in its Father's arms. 'Whoever is a *little one*, let him come to me.' So speaks the Holy Spirit through Solomon. This same Spirit of Love also says: '*For to him that is little, mercy will be shown.*' The Prophet Isaiah reveals in His name that on the last day: '*God shall feed his flock like a shepherd; he shall gather together the lambs*

---

[13] Chiara Lubich, 'Word of Life', July 2005.

with his arm and shall take them up in his bosom.' As though these promises were not sufficient, this same prophet whose gaze was already plunged into the eternal depths cried out in the Lord's name: *'As one whom his mother caresses, so I will comfort you; you shall be carried at the breasts and upon the knees they will caress you.'*

After having listened to words such as these, dear godmother, there is nothing to do but to be silent and weep with gratitude and love. Ah! If all weak and imperfect souls felt what the least of souls feels, that is, the soul of your little Thérèse, not one would despair of reaching the summit of the mount of love. Jesus does not demand great actions from us but simply *surrender* and *gratitude*. Has He not said: *'I will take the he-goats from out your flocks, for all the beasts of the forest are mine, the cattle on the hills and the oxen. I know all the fowls of the air. If I were hungry, I would not tell you, for the world is mine, and the fullness thereof. Shall I eat the flesh of bulls or drink the blood of goats? OFFER TO GOD THE SACRIFICES OF PRAISE AND THANKSGIVING.'*

See then all that Jesus lays claim to from us; He has no need of our works but only of our love, for the same God who declares He *has no need to tell us when He is hungry* did not fear *to beg* for a little water from the Samaritan woman. He was thirsty. But when He said: *'Give me a drink'*, it was the *love* of the poor creature the Creator of the universe was seeking. He was thirsty for love. Ah! I feel it more than ever before, Jesus is *parched*, for He meets only the ungrateful and indifferent among His disciples in the world, and among *His own disciples*, alas, He finds few hearts who surrender to Him without reservations, who understand the real tenderness of His infinite love.

Story of a Soul, Manuscript B, Chapter 9, pages 192–3

To be Your Spouse, to be a Carmelite, and by my union with You to be the Mother of souls, should not this suffice me? And yet it is not so. No doubt, these three privileges sum up my true *vocation: Carmelite, Spouse, Mother,* and yet I feel within me other vocations. I feel the *vocation* of the WARRIOR, THE PRIEST, THE APOSTLE, THE DOCTOR, THE MARTYR. Finally, I feel the need and the desire of carrying out the most heroic deeds for *You, O Jesus.* I feel within my soul the courage of the *Crusader,* the *Papal Guard,* and I would want to die on the field of battle in defence of the Church.

I feel within me the *vocation* of the PRIEST. With what love, O Jesus, I would carry You in my hands when, at my voice, You would come down from heaven. And with what love I would give you to souls! But alas! While desiring to be a *Priest,* I admire and envy the humility of St Francis of Assisi and I feel the vocation of imitating him in refusing the sublime dignity of the *Priesthood.*

O Jesus, my Love, my Life, how can I combine these contrasts? How can I realise the desires of my poor *little soul?*

Ah! In spite of my littleness, I would like to enlighten souls as did the Prophets and the Doctors. I have the *vocation of the Apostle.* I would like to travel over the whole earth to preach Your Name and plant Your glorious Cross on infidel soil. But *O my Beloved,* one mission would not be sufficient for me, I would want to preach the Gospel on all five continents simultaneously and even to the remotest isles. I would be a missionary, not for a few years only, but from the beginning of creation until the consummation of the ages. But above all, O my Beloved Saviour, I would shed my blood for You even to the very last drop.

Story of a Soul, **Manuscript B, Chapter 9, pages 193–4**

During my meditation, my desires caused me a veritable martyrdom, and I opened the Epistles of St Paul to find some kind of answer. Chapters 12 and 13 of the First Epistle to the Corinthians fell under my eyes. I read there, in the first of these chapters, that *all* cannot be apostles, prophets, doctors, etc., that the Church is composed of different members, and that the eye cannot be the hand at *one and the same time.* The answer was clear, but it did not fulfil my desires and gave me no peace. But just as Mary Magdalen always found what she was seeking by always stooping down and looking into the empty tomb, so I, abasing myself to the very depths of my nothingness, raised myself so high that I was able to attain my end. Without becoming discouraged, I continued my reading, and this sentence consoled me: *'Yet strive after the BETTER GIFTS, and I point out to you a yet more excellent way.'* And the Apostle explains how all *the most PERFECT gifts* are nothing without *LOVE. That Charity is the EXCELLENT WAY that leads most surely to* God.

I finally had rest. Considering the mystical body of the Church, I had not recognised myself in any of the members described by St Paul, or rather I had desired to see myself in them *all. Charity* gave me the key to my *vocation.* I understood that if the Church had a body composed of different members, the most necessary and the most noble of all could not be lacking to it, and so I understood that the Church *had a Heart and that this Heart* was BURNING WITH LOVE. I understood that it was Love alone that made the Church's members act, that if Love ever became extinct, apostles would not preach the Gospel and martyrs would not shed their blood. I understood that LOVE COMPRISED ALL VOCATIONS, THAT IT EMBRACED ALL TIMES AND PLACES ... IN A WORD, THAT IT WAS ETERNAL!

Then, in the excess of my delirious joy, I cried out: O Jesus, my Love ... my *vocation*, at last I have found it ... MY VOCATION IS LOVE!

Yes, I have found my place in the Church and it is You, O my God, who have given me this place; in the heart of the Church, my Mother, I shall be *Love*. Thus I shall be everything, and thus my dream will be realised.

CHAPTER SEVEN

Saint Edith Stein

'The Prayer of the Church'

Edith Stein was born on 12 October 1891 in Breslau, which was then in Germany, but is now in Poland and called Wrocław.[1] She was the youngest of the seven surviving children born to Siegfried and Auguste Stein. Theirs was a devout Jewish family. Siegfried died when Edith was only two years old. Her mother took over the management of Siegfried's lumber business. This was a difficult task, but Auguste succeeded because she had a very strong faith in God, and she was good with people.

Edith was small and frail as a child, and rather stubborn, but from the age of seven she realised that her mother and older sister Frieda knew what was best for her and she decided to obey them. At school she excelled at languages, adding Greek, English, French and Dutch to her native German. Her favourite language was Latin. She loved the terseness of Latin, how it could express so much in so few words.

In 1906, at the age of fifteen, Edith decided that she wanted a break from school and went to live with

[1] A good account of St Edith's life is to be found in *Edith Stein: The Life and Legacy of St. Teresa Benedicta of the Cross* by María Ruiz Scaperlanda (Manchester, New Hampshire: Sophia Institute Press, 2017).

her sister Else and brother-in-law Max in Hamburg. She helped with the housework and with looking after their three small children. During this time, she stopped praying and, according to her own account, became an atheist. The following year she returned home and resumed her studies. From 1911 to 1913 Edith attended the university in Breslau where she studied Philosophy, Psychology, History and German Philology.

Philosophy was what interested Edith most, because she was searching for the truth. She was particularly drawn to the thought of Professor Edmund Husserl and his philosophy of phenomenology. Put simply, phenomenology holds that there is a real world out there: real things and real people. This was a reaction to much of European philosophy since the seventeenth century which held that we could only know ideas. In 1913, Edith moved to Göttingen to study under Edmund Husserl. In 1914 the First World War broke out and Edith volunteered to work with the Red Cross. She was assigned to a hospital for infectious diseases in the Carpathian Mountains, where she worked as a nurse's assistant for most of 1915.

In 1916 Husserl moved to Freiburg and Edith, released from her duties in the hospital, went there also in order to finish her doctorate. She presented her dissertation 'On the Problem of Empathy' and did her oral examinations later that year. In March 1917, Edith was conferred with the degree of Doctor of Philosophy *summa cum laude*. Husserl took Edith on as his assistant, but she found that this work, which was mainly secretarial, did not give her enough scope to exercise her own creativity. She wanted to become a lecturer in the university, but she was advised that they would not employ a woman in that role. Edith returned home and continued her studies privately. During this time, she spent a good deal of time visiting the friends she knew from university, often staying for periods in their homes. This was also the period when her search for truth was gradually leading her back to faith in God.

Edith grew up in a devout Jewish family, and even though she turned away from belief in God in her teenage years, that formation was always there. When she rediscovered faith in God as a Christian, the Jewish foundation reasserted itself. Edith's awakening to Christian faith was gradual. It came about through the influence of the intellectual circles in which she moved when she was a university student. All her friends were believers – Jewish, Protestant or Catholic – as were her professors. Her mentor Husserl was Lutheran. Max Scheler, whose work she admired, was Catholic.

The tipping point came one night when Edith was staying in a friend's house and could not sleep. She went downstairs to find something to read. The *Life* of St Teresa of Ávila came to hand. It was like the *tolle lege* (take up and read) moment in St Augustine's *Confessions* when the dam broke and what had been building up for some time broke through. Edith stayed up all night reading St Teresa's autobiography. When she put it down, she said: 'This is the truth.' She decided then to join the Catholic Church.

Edith was baptised and received First Holy Communion in the parish church of St Martin in Breslau on 1 January 1922. She was confirmed by the Bishop of Speyer in his private chapel on 2 February. She took the name Theresia Hedwig but continued to be known as Edith. From the start, Edith was attracted to the Carmelite vocation, as St Teresa of Ávila had been instrumental in bringing her into the Church. However, one shock was probably enough for Edith's mother. In any case, her spiritual director, Monsignor Josef Schwind, advised her that she was not ready for this further step and that she should live the Christian life in the world for some years first.

In 1923, Edith secured a position as a lecturer in the Teachers' College in Speyer, a college for the training of women teachers run by Dominican Sisters. She got rooms adjacent to the nuns' quarters and was able to attend Mass and the Divine Office daily. She led a quasi-monastic life during her time in Speyer. During her years there she was a frequent guest and retreatant at the Benedictine monastery of Beuron. The Liturgical Movement was flourishing at the time and Beuron was one of its main centres. Edith came to appreciate the liturgy as a source of spirituality. She had a unique perspective on the liturgy, because with her Jewish background she was able to see how the Christian liturgy grew out of the Jewish liturgy. When Monsignor Schwind died in 1927, the Archabbot of Beuron, Dom Raphael Walzer, became her spiritual director.

During her years in Speyer, Edith was well liked by her students as she gave them personal attention. She also continued her academic work translating works by Cardinal Newman (now St John Henry Newman) and St Thomas Aquinas into German. She attended conferences and gave public lectures, especially to Catholic women's associations. Many of her lectures were also published as essays.

In 1932 Edith moved to Münster to lecture at the German Institute for Scientific Pedagogy. However, the following year Adolf Hitler came to power in Germany and enacted anti-Semitic laws which resulted in Edith losing her job in the institute. She took this as the definitive sign that it was now the will of God that she should enter Carmel.

Edith entered the Cologne Carmel on 14 October 1933. She received the habit on 15 April 1934. She took the name Teresa Benedicta of the Cross, combining the Carmelite and Benedictine influences with her premonition that the cross would mark her life in a particular way. She was known in the convent as Sister Benedicta. She made her final profession of vows in April 1938. During her years in Carmel, her religious superiors encouraged her to continue writing and occasionally the prioress asked her to give a talk to the nuns. Some of Edith's meditations on the cross were shared with the community on the Feast of the Holy Cross, when the nuns renewed their vows.

By the end of 1938, the situation of Jews in Germany had become more dangerous. Edith's sister Rosa, who had also become a Catholic, had come to live at the convent without becoming a nun. It was decided that it would be safer if both Edith and Rosa moved to the Carmel in Echt in the Netherlands. There was a possibility that Edith could have gone to Switzerland, but then she would have had to leave Rosa behind. However, the Netherlands turned out to be no safer than Germany, as it was invaded by the Nazi forces in May 1940. On 2 August 1942 Edith and Rosa were seized by the Gestapo and transported to Auschwitz where they perished in the gas chamber on 9 August.

Edith Stein's published works include her doctoral thesis *On the Problem of Empathy,* other philosophical works including *Finite and Eternal Being* and *Philosophy of Psychology and the Humanities.* She was interested in the role of women in society and in the Church. Many of her lectures to women's groups were later published as *Essays on Woman.* Her religious writings include *Knowledge and Faith, The Mystery of Christmas* and *The Science of the Cross.* Edith left an unfinished autobiographical work entitled *Life in a Jewish Family.* Her many letters also give an insight into her personal life. Many of Edith's spiritual reflections have been collected and published in *The Hidden Life: Essays, Meditations, Spiritual Texts.* It is from this collection that I have selected her essay 'The Prayer of the Church' as a significant piece of writing that will give us an insight into Edith Stein's spirituality.

The Prayer of the Church

Saint Teresa of Ávila and St John of the Cross have very little to say about the liturgy. Their interest was in personal prayer and, although they mention Holy Communion and occasionally quote a psalm which was in the Divine Office, the liturgy was not seen by them as a major source of prayer. In the Church of their day, liturgy and spirituality were seen as separate and having little influence on each other. This was mainly because the liturgy was in Latin, a language that was not understood by most people, including religious, unless they were priests. Even those who did have a knowledge of Latin could only follow the Mass with difficulty, as the Low Mass, which was the form of the celebration usually used, was said in a low voice by the priest, so that the people could not hear what he was saying. In contrast to the great Spanish Carmelite doctors, Edith Stein has much to say about the liturgy. This is because she was influenced by the Liturgical Movement.

The Liturgical Movement sought to make the liturgy accessible to the people and make it central to spirituality and the life of the Church. The Liturgical Movement began as part of a revival of monastic life in France, Germany and Belgium in the nineteenth century. Dom Prosper Guéranger, who re-founded the Abbey of Solesmes in France in 1833, put the liturgy at the heart of the daily life of the monastery. Dom Guéranger's great insight was that the liturgical year was the Church's great catechesis. In the first millennium there was no other catechesis and it was very effective. Dom Guéranger also wanted to restore Gregorian chant as the proper music of the Roman Rite. In Germany the Abbey of Beuron was re-founded by the brothers Maurus and Placidus Wolter with the help of Princess Catherine von Hohenzollern in 1863. They were inspired by what was happening in Solesmes.

What began in monasteries quickly had an influence on the secular clergy and parishes, as monasteries like Solemnes, Beuron and their daughter houses organised conferences for priests and published books and periodicals on the subject of the liturgy. In 1883 the Abbey of Maria Laach brought out a Missal giving the text of the liturgy in Latin with a vernacular translation in parallel columns to help the faithful follow the Mass. In 1903 St Pius X issued the motu proprio *Tra le sollecitudini* in which he encouraged the active participation of the faithful in the liturgy and proposed the use of Gregorian chant for congregational singing. In 1909, at a Catholic congress in Mechelen (Malines) in Belgium, Dom Lambert Beauduin called for the involvement of the people in the liturgy as a pastoral priority. The Liturgical Movement gained momentum after that and ultimately led to the reform of the liturgy by the Second Vatican Council. In Germany the Benedictines promoted research into the history of the liturgy and study of the early sources. Many theologians, including Romano Guardini and Dom Odo Casel, contributed to the theology of the liturgy.[2] All of this was one of the important currents in the life of the Church in Germany when Edith was received into the Church in 1922.

There were three influences in Edith Stein's spirituality. These were the Jewish foundation, the Benedictine liturgical formation and the Carmelite tradition of contemplative prayer. She saw liturgy and contemplation as two complementary aspects of the one life of prayer. In her essay 'The Prayer of the Church', Edith Stein shows that both the liturgy and contemplation are participations in the prayer of Christ and of his body the Church. Edith was very

---

[2] Cf. Johannes H. Emminghaus, *The Eucharist: Essence, Form, Celebration* (Collegeville: The Liturgical Press, 1997), pp. 90–4.

conscious that Jesus was a Jew and prayed as a Jew. He would have said the customary prayers in the home with Mary and Joseph and he went to Jerusalem for the great pilgrimage feasts. Edith examines the Last Supper in the light of this.

> From his last supper with his disciples, we know that Jesus said the old blessings over bread, wine, and the fruits of the earth, as they are prayed to this day.[3]

Edith was familiar with these blessings from her own upbringing. She goes on to recall the institution of the Eucharist. Edith was able to connect the Eucharist of the Last Supper with the Jewish Passover because of her own experience of celebrating the Passover in her family. When Edith was writing, most Catholics would have been unaware of the Jewish roots of the Eucharist. They would have assumed that Jesus invented the whole rite rather than taking an existing rite and giving it new meaning. Edith explains this as follows.

> Blessing and distributing bread and wine are part of the Passover rite. But here both receive an entirely new meaning.... In the mouth of Christ, the old blessings become life-giving words. The fruits of the earth become his body and blood, filled with his life. Visible creation, which he entered when he became a human being, is now united with him in a new, mysterious way.[4]

---

[3] Edith Stein, 'The Prayer of the Church' in *The Collected Works of Edith Stein*, Vol. 4, *The Hidden Life: Essays, Meditations, Spiritual Texts*, edited by Dr. L. Gelber and Michael Linssen OCD, translated by Waltraut Stein, PhD (Washington: ICS Publications, 1992, 2014), p. 7.

[4] Ibid., p. 8.

When approached in this way, the nature of the Eucharist as a meal also becomes clear.

> Through the Lord's last supper, the Passover meal of the Old Covenant is converted into the Easter meal of the New Covenant: into the sacrifice on the cross at Golgotha and those joyous meals between Easter and Ascension when the disciples recognised the Lord in the breaking of bread, and into the sacrifice of the Mass with Holy Communion.[5]

It was one of the achievements of the Liturgical Movement to have reintegrated the ideas of meal and sacrifice which had tended to be separated in the theology and spirituality of the Post-Tridentine period. The Council of Trent had dealt with the Sacrifice of the Mass and the Sacrament of Holy Communion in two separate sessions. Subsequently, they were treated as separate topics in manuals of theology.

Edith goes on to discuss the Eucharist as thanksgiving. The whole of Christ's life was an act of thanksgiving to the Father for creation, for redemption, for what God is doing in the world. Christ gathers and unites the whole of creation with and in himself in a great offering of thanksgiving and praise. Again, we see the influence of Edith's Jewish background where 'blessing' always includes thanksgiving as well as petition.

> Some understanding of this eucharistic character of prayer had already been revealed under the Old Covenant. The wonderous form of the tent of meeting, and later, of Solomon's temple, erected as it was according to divine

---

[5] Edith Stein, 'The Prayer of the Church', p. 8.

specifications, was considered an image of the entire creation, assembled in worship and service around the Lord.[6]

In the place of Solomon's Temple, Christ has built a temple of living stones – his body the Church. He himself is the high priest. The whole of creation is drawn into the liturgy. The earthly liturgy is united with the heavenly liturgy in which the angels and saints praise the Blessed Trinity forever.

> When these [the Christian people] stream into cathedrals and chapels on holy days, when they joyously participate daily in worship using the 'people's choral Mass' and the new 'folk Mass' forms, they show that they are conscious of their calling to praise God. The liturgical unity of the heavenly with the earthly church, both of which thank God 'through Christ,' finds its most powerful expression in the preface and Sanctus of the Mass.[7]

In the passage above, Edith is referring to some of the early attempts to involve the people in the prayers of the Mass. In the 'people's choral Mass' the congregation sang metrical versions of such parts of the Mass as the *Gloria*, *Sanctus* and *Agnus Dei* in German while the priest recited them quietly in Latin. 'Folk' does not refer to music, but to the German word *volk* meaning people. In the 'dialogue Mass' (as it was known in France) the people recited the responses in Latin. Previously, these had only been said by the altar servers. These initiatives were directly inspired by the Liturgical Movement.

---

[6] Edith Stein, 'The Prayer of the Church', p. 9.
[7] Ibid., p. 10.

Having discussed Our Lord's participation in the Jewish liturgy and its transformation into the Christian liturgy, Edith goes on to discuss the solitary prayer of Jesus, to which there are many references in the Gospels. At the start of his ministry, Jesus spent forty days in the desert praying alone. Before he chose the apostles, he spent the night in prayer and he frequently went to a lonely place to pray. Do we know anything of the content of this prayer? Edith says that the prayer of Jesus in the garden on the Mount of Olives is like a flash of lightening, giving us a momentary glimpse into the intimate conversation of Jesus with God the Father. She goes on to say that there is one occasion when Jesus allowed the disciples to listen in to the secret dialogue. This was a little earlier on the same evening. The prayer is recorded for us in Chapter 17 of St John's Gospel. In this prayer, Edith also sees a connection with the Old Covenant.

> We call these words Jesus' high priestly prayer, for this talking alone with God also had its antecedent in the Old Covenant. Once a year on the greatest and most holy day of the year, on the Day of Atonement, the high priest stepped into the Holy of Holies before the face of the Lord 'to pray for himself and his household and the whole congregation of Israel'.[8]

The Day of Atonement, *Yom Kippur*, had a special significance for Edith: it was her birthday. Her mother Auguste regarded having a baby on that day as a sign of God's special blessing. Edith came to see it also as a reminder of the Cross, because, as she explains in her essay, the Day of Atonement is the antecedent of Good Friday. All the elaborate details of the ritual

---

[8] Edith Stein, 'The Prayer of the Church', pp. 11–12.

prescribed in the Book of Leviticus find their fulfilment in the events of Good Friday. The ram that was slaughtered as a sin offering for the people represents the Lamb of God. The scapegoat who symbolically carried the sins of the people prefigures Christ carrying his cross. Edith goes through the various details of the ceremony.

> And the high priest descended from Aaron foreshadows the eternal high priest. Just as Christ anticipated his sacrificial death during the last supper, so he also anticipated the high priestly prayer ... He did not have to await the hour prescribed by the Law, nor to seek out the Holy of Holies in the temple. He stands, always and everywhere before the face of God; his own soul is the Holy of Holies.[9]

What does this prayer reveal to us? Edith tells us that it shows us that the three Divine Persons in the Blessed Trinity dwell in each other. It reveals a relationship. She sees the prayer of Christ as essentially consisting in silence.

> The Saviour's high priestly prayer unveils the mystery of the inner life: the circumincession of the Divine Persons and the indwelling of God in the soul. In these mysterious depths the work of salvation was prepared and accomplished itself in concealment and silence.[10]

Edith goes on to discuss the importance of solitary, silent prayer. She gives many examples. The Blessed Virgin Mary conceived the Word in silence. It was in solitary prayer that Saul (St Paul) received his mission.

---

[9] Edith Stein, 'The Prayer of the Church', p. 12.
[10] Ibid.

Similarly, St Peter was prepared for the admission of the Gentiles to the Church during a vision received during prayer alone. We do not know how much the course of history has been influenced by the prayer of the saints down through the ages. Edith mentions St Bridget of Sweden, St Catherine of Siena and St Teresa of Ávila. It is interesting to note that Edith now shares the title Patroness of Europe with Bridget and Catherine. For Edith, the silent dialogue with God is also the prayer of the Church. It makes us available to the Lord for the building up of his kingdom.

Dialogue with Chiara Lubich

Chiara Lubich saw Edith Stein as having contributed to reconciliation between people of different faiths and so helped to shape a more inclusive and united society in Europe. In an address to a conference of European mayors in November 2001, Chiara said the following:

> And then with Edith Stein, nearly our contemporary, holiness descended into the depths of the horror that overwhelmed Europe. In her personal sacrifice she gave witness to a dual faithfulness: to her people and to her faith. She died as a Christian nun, but she died because she was Jewish. Thus, she set the cornerstone of a 'European home' in which all religions can cooperate in building brotherhood.[11]

---

[11] Chiara Lubich, *Essential Writings*, p. 250.

Readings for *Lectio Divina*

'The Prayer of the Church', Extract
(*The Collected Works of Edith Stein*, Volume 4, pages 8–9)

Blessing and distributing bread and wine are part of the Passover rite. But here both receive an entirely new meaning. This is where the life of the church begins. Only at Pentecost will it appear publicly as a Spirit-filled and visible community. But here at the Passover meal the seeds of the vineyard are planted that make the outpouring of the Spirit possible. In the mouth of Christ, the old blessings become life-giving words. The fruits of the earth become his body and blood, filled with his life. Visible creation, which he entered when he became a human being, is now united with him in a new, mysterious way. The things that serve to sustain human life are fundamentally transformed, and the people who partake of them in faith are transformed too, drawn into the unity of life with Christ and filled with his divine life. The Word's life-giving power is bound to the sacrifice. The Word became flesh in order to surrender the life he assumed, to offer himself and a creation redeemed by his sacrifice in praise to the Creator. Through the Lord's last supper, the Passover meal of the Old Covenant is converted into the Easter meal of the New Covenant: into the sacrifice on the cross at Golgotha and those joyous meals between Easter and Ascension when the disciples recognised the Lord in the breaking of bread, and into the sacrifice of the Mass with Holy Communion.

As the Lord took the cup, he gave thanks. This recalls the words of blessing thanking the Creator. But we also know that Christ used to give thanks when, prior to a miracle, he raised his eyes to his Father in heaven. He gives thanks because he knows in advance that he will be heard. He gives thanks for the divine power that he carries in himself and by means of which he will demonstrate the omnipotence of the Creator to human eyes. He gives thanks for the work of salvation that he is permitted to accomplish, and through this work, which is in fact the glorification of the triune Godhead, because it restores this Godhead's distorted image to pure beauty. Therefore, the whole perpetual sacrificial offering of Christ – at the cross, in the holy Mass, and in the eternal glory of heaven – can be conceived as a single great thanksgiving – as Eucharist: as gratitude for creation, salvation, and consummation. Christ presents himself in the name of all creation, whose prototype he is and to which he descended to renew it from the inside out and lead it to perfection. But he also calls upon the entire created world itself, united with him, to give the Creator the tribute of thanks that is his due.

'The Prayer of the Church', Extract
(*The Collected Works of Edith Stein*, Volume 4, pages 9–10)

In place of Solomon's temple, Christ has built a temple of living stones, the communion of saints. At its centre, he stands as the eternal high priest; on its altar he is himself the perpetual sacrifice. And, in turn, the whole of creation is drawn into the 'liturgy', the ceremonial worship service: the fruits of the earth as the mysterious offerings, the flowers and the lighted candlesticks, the carpets and the curtain, the ordained priest, and the anointing and blessing of God's house. Even the cherubim are not missing. Fashioned by the hand of the artist, the visible forms stand watch beside the Holy of Holies. And, as living copies of them, the 'monks resembling angels' surround the sacrificial altar and make sure that the praise of God does not cease as in heaven so on earth. The solemn prayers they recite as the resonant mouth of the church frame the holy sacrifice. They also frame, permeate, and consecrate all other 'daily work', so that prayer and work become a single *opus Dei*, a single 'liturgy'. Their readings from the Holy Scriptures and from the fathers, from the church's menologies and the teachings of its principal pastors, are a great, continually swelling hymn of praise to the rule of providence and to the progressive actualisation of the eternal plan of salvation. Their morning hymns of praise call all of creation together to unite once more in praising the Lord: mountains and hills, streams and rivers, seas and lands and all that inhabit them, clouds and winds, rain and snow, all peoples of earth, every class and race of people, and finally also the inhabitants of heaven, the angels and the saints. Not only in representations giving them human form and made by human hands are they to participate in the great Eucharist of creation, but they are to be involved as personal beings – or better, we are to unite ourselves through our liturgy to their eternal praise of God.

'The Prayer of the Church', Extract
(*The Collected Works of Edith Stein,* Volume 4, pages 11–13)

Christ prayed interiorly not only when he had withdrawn from the crowd, but also when he was among people. And once he allowed us to look extensively and deeply at this secret dialogue. It was not long before the hour of the Mount of Olives; in fact, it was immediately before they set out to go there at the end of the last supper, which we recognise as the actual hour of the birth of the church. 'Having loved his own ..., he loved them to the end.' He knew that this was their last time together, and he wanted to give them as much as he in any way could. He had to restrain himself from saying more. But he surely knew that they could not bear any more, in fact, that they could not even grasp this little bit. The Spirit of Truth had to come first to open their eyes for it. And after he had said and done all that he could say and do, he lifted his eyes to heaven and spoke to the Father in their presence.

The Saviour's high priestly prayer unveils the mystery of the inner life: the circumincession of the Divine Persons and the indwelling of God in the soul. In these mysterious depths the work of salvation was prepared and accomplished itself in concealment and silence. And so it will continue until the union of all is actually accomplished at the end of time. The decision for the Redemption was conceived in the eternal silence of the inner divine life. The power of the Holy Spirit came over the Virgin praying alone in the hidden, silent room in Nazareth and brought about the Incarnation of the Saviour. Congregated around the silently praying Virgin, the emergent church awaited the promised new outpouring of the Spirit that was to quicken it into clarity and fruitful outer effectiveness. In the night of blindness that God had laid over his eyes, Saul awaited in solitary prayer the Lord's answer to his question, 'What do you want me to do?' In solitary prayer Peter was prepared for his mission to the Gentiles. And so it has remained all through the centuries. In silent dialogue with their Lord of souls consecrated to God, the events of church history are prepared that, visible far and wide, renew the face of the earth. The Virgin, who kept every word sent from God in her heart, is the model for such attentive souls in whom Jesus' high priestly prayer comes to life again and again.

Select Bibliography

Brother Lawrence of the Resurrection, *The Practice of the Presence of God,* Critical Edition by Conrad De Meester OCD, translated by Salvatore Sciurba OCD (Washington: ICS Publications, 1994).

Emminghaus, J.H., *The Eucharist: Essence, Form Celebration* (Collegeville: The Liturgical Press, 1997).

Saint John of the Cross, *The Collected Works of St John of the Cross,* translated by Kieran Kavanaugh OCD and Otilio Rodriguez OCD (Washington: ICS Publications, 1991).

Saint Teresa of Ávila, *The Collected Works of Saint Teresa of Avila,* translated by Kieran Kavanaugh OCD and Otilio Rodriguez OCD, Volume 1, Second Edition (Washington: ICS Publications, 1987).

Saint Teresa of Ávila, *The Collected Works of Saint Teresa of Avila,* translated by Kieran Kavanaugh OCD and Otilio Rodriguez OCD, Volume 2 (Washington: ICS Publications, 1980).

Saint Thérèse of Lisieux, *Her Last Conversations,* translated from the Original Manuscripts by John Clark OCD (Washington: ICS Publications, 1977).

Saint Thérèse of Lisieux, *Letters of St. Thérèse of Lisieux,* General Correspondence translated from the Original Manuscripts by John Clarke OCD, Volume 2 (Washington: ICS Publications, 1988).

Saint Thérèse of Lisieux, *Story of a Soul: The Autobiography of St Thérèse of Lisieux*, translated from the Original Manuscripts by John Clarke OCD, Third Edition (Washington: ICS Publications, 1996).

Scaperlanda, M.R., *Edith Stein: The Life and Legacy of St Teresa Benedicta of the Cross* (Manchester, New Hampshire: Sophia Institute Press, 2017).

Stein, E., *The Collected Works of Edith Stein*, Volume 4: *The Hidden Life: Essays, Meditations, Spiritual Texts*, edited by Dr L. Gelber and Michael Linssen OCD, translated by Waltraut Stein PhD (Washington: ICS Publications, 1992, 2014).

Lubich, C., *Essential Writings*, compiled and edited by Michael Vandeleene (London: New City Press, 2007).

Lubich, C., *Meditations* (London: New City Press, 1975).

Lubich, C., *The Art of Loving* (New York: New City Press, 2010).

Lubich, C., 'The Word of Life', published monthly by the Focolare Movement, Prosperous, Co. Kildare.